THE EXPLORATION OF SOUTH AMERICA

THEMES IN EUROPEAN EXPANSION: EXPLORATION,
COLONIZATION, AND THE IMPACT OF EMPIRE
(General Editor: James A. Casada)
Vol. 4

GARLAND REFERENCE LIBRARY
OF SOCIAL SCIENCE
(Vol. 148)

THE EXPLORATION OF SOUTH AMERICA
An Annotated Bibliography

Edward J. Goodman

GARLAND PUBLISHING, INC. • NEW YORK & LONDON
1983

© 1983 Edward J. Goodman
All rights reserved

Library of Congress Cataloging in Publication Data

Goodman, Edward J. (Edward Julius), 1916–
 The exploration of South America.

 (Themes in European expansion : exploration,
colonization, and the impact of empire ; vol. 4)
(Garland reference library of social science ; vol. 148)
 Includes indexes.
 1. America—Discovery and exploration—Bibliography.
2. South America—History—To 1806—Bibliography.
I. Title. II. Series: Themes in European expansion ;
v. 4. III. Series: Garland reference library of social science ; v. 148.
Z1212.G66 1983 [E101]   016.980′01   82-49177
ISBN 0-8240-9180-9

Printed on acid-free, 250-year-life paper
Manufactured in the United States of America

To Charles E. Nowell

CONTENTS

Editor's Introduction	ix
Introduction	xiii
I. Bibliographical Guides	3
II. Collections of Documents	5
III. Collections of Contemporary Accounts	9
IV. General Background	13
A. Exploration in General	13
B. Geography and Cartography	18
C. General Histories of the Indies	20
D. Histories of Specific Areas	23
E. Myths and Legends	27
V. Fifteenth- and Sixteenth-Century Exploration	29
A. Early Discoveries and Exploration	29
B. The Great Discoverers	32
C. Early Discoveries	43
1. Brazil	43
2. The Amazon Region	50
3. The Northern Coasts	51
4. Southeastern South America	55
5. The Pacific Coast	58
D. The Conquest and the Late Sixteenth Century	60
1. General	60
2. The Amazon Region	61
3. Northern South America	62
4. Southern South America	66
5. The West Coast	69
VI. Seventeenth- and Eighteenth-Century Exploration	73
A. Exploration in General	73
B. Eastern South America	73

1. Brazil in General	73
2. The Amazon Region	74
3. The *Bandeirantes* and the *Monções*	76
4. Northern South America	77
5. Western South America	78
6. Southern South America	79
C. The Missionary Explorers	82
D. Scientific Exploration	87
VII. Nineteenth- and Twentieth-Century Exploration	97
A. Nineteenth-Century Exploration in General	97
B. The Great Naturalists	109
C. Nineteenth-Century Scientific Exploration: Privately Sponsored	124
D. Nineteenth-Century Scientific Exploration: Government Sponsored	130
E. Twentieth-Century Exploration	143
ADDENDA	153
AUTHOR INDEX	157
TOPICAL INDEX	167

SERIES EDITOR'S INTRODUCTION

The author of the third volume in the series "Themes in European Expansion: Exploration, Colonization, and the Impact of Empire," Edward J. Goodman, is emeritus professor of history at Xavier University in Cincinnati, Ohio. He received his A.B. from Loras College in 1938 and an M.A. degree from Columbia University the following year. Goodman then served briefly as an instructor of history at Notre Dame College, Staten Island, New York, before entering the United States Army Air Forces during World War II. Following the war's conclusion he returned to academic life, teaching for one term at Seton Hall University before becoming an assistant professor at the United States Naval Academy, a position he held for four years. During the same period Goodman was completing requirements for his Ph.D., which he received from Columbia University in 1951. Shortly before earning the doctorate he moved to Xavier University. In the intervening years Goodman rose through the ranks to professor of history. He also has held visiting professorships at the Catholic University of America and at the University of Illinois-Urbana.

Goodman enjoys a firmly established reputation as one of this country's outstanding authorities on the discovery and exploration of South America. He has travelled widely in Europe and South America in connection with his researches, and he has held fellowships for work on French explorers in South America and on the career of Alexander von Humboldt. His efforts have resulted in an impressive array of talks, papers, and publications. Among the latter have been contributions to various learned journals, encyclopedias, textbooks, and anthologies. Goodman is the editor of *The United States and Latin America Look at Each Other* (1959) and *Colombia, Ecuador, and Venezuela: Their Peoples and Economies Today and Tomorrow* (1960). However, his most important work of a scholarship is *The Explorers of South America* (1972), a standard source on the subject. Presently he is preparing two further book-length manuscripts on "The New World of Alexander von Humboldt" and "After Lewis and Clark: The Explorers of North America Since 1806." While he has retired from teaching (residing now in Fort Myers, Florida), Goodman's ongoing writing and research efforts typify those of a committed and active scholar. In short, the present work is a product from an accomplished authority who brings upwards of three decades of experience and expertise to his task. The result is an invaluable reference tool for a neglected yet increasingly important part of the world. As such, it is a welcome addition to this series.

The Exploration of South America: A Bibliography fills a significant gap in the existing reference literature on the continent. As Goodman points out in his fine bibliographical essay introducing the book, heretofore we have had nothing approaching a comprehensive guide to the literature in the field. Yet today South America looms perhaps larger than ever before in American foreign policy, and all of us are cognizant of the uncertainty, not to mention official mistakes, that have characterized our government's official approaches to the region in the recent past. These considerations, in and of themselves, are sufficient to suggest the need for a fuller understanding of the South American past and the factors which historically have contributed to its present situation. The comprehensive coverage of the literature treating Europe and the wider world's initial contacts with the continent offered in Goodman's work marks a logical starting point for such an understanding.

Equally important, although in a somewhat different vein, is the book's utilitarian value to academicians in a variety of fields. It fills a major void, bibliographically speaking, in Latin American studies. Inasmuch as such studies form a part of the course offerings in virtually every four-year college and university in the United States, not to mention similar institutions elsewhere in the world, this book should become an indispensable part of their reference collections. Also, it promises to be something of a milestone for students of historical geography, travel literature, and discovery and exploration. Perhaps no other continent or major geographical region is presently so well served in a bibli-

Series Editor's Introduction

ographical sense. Finally, general users will find the work, thanks to its fine indexing and careful annotation, a ready guide to both the established authorities in the field of South American exploration and to those intrepid adventurers who made the continent known to a wider world. For all the foregoing reasons, this book should be hailed with gratitude, and certainly it nicely compliments its predecessor volumes in the series.

James A. Casada
Winthrop College

INTRODUCTION

The publication of an increasing number of significant books and articles relating to the discovery and exploration of South America give ample evidence of a growing interest in this particular field of study. Despite this fact, no comprehensive bibliography has as yet appeared to apprise the interested scholar or general reader of the number, scope, and nature of the writings on this subject. Up to now the only bibliographical resources available have been the sections on discovery and exploration in the *Guide to Historical Literature* (both the original and the new editions), in *Latin America: a Guide to the Historical Literature* (like the previous guides chiefly concerned with the great age of discovery), and in the bibliographies of such recent works as Samuel Eliot Morison's *The European Discovery of America: The Southern Voyages*, J. H. Parry's *The Discovery of South America* (both of which are limited to the fifteenth and sixteenth centuries), the article "South America" in Helen Delpar's *The Discoverers*, and in my *The Explorers of South America* which, although it covers five centuries, is limited to works cited in the text. The present work is an effort to fill the need for a more extensive bibliography of the entire period of the discovery and exploration of the continent.

Few areas of world history can offer more drama than the history of the discovery and exploration of South America. The setting itself is extraordinary—a vast, hitherto unknown continent, containing some of the greatest river systems in the world, the most extensive mountain system (highest in the western hemisphere), high, windswept plateaus, and forbidding deserts. It was the home of millions of aborigines whose cultural level ranged from primitive savagery to the high civilization of the Incas, and who were proof of the ability of man to survive in almost any climate and under the most trying conditions. To most of the *Conquistadores* they were a vast labor pool; to missionaries of incredible valor and endurance, they were a harvest of souls to be found and baptized. There were also the exotic flora and fauna that would so interest naturalists, and the vast wealth in gold, silver, and precious stones that dazzled the conquerors and led men to perform unbelievable feats in the effort to find and acquire them. And as if reality were not enough, there were also persistent tales of gold and silver cities, and of lost cities for which men would risk and lose their lives in a vain search.

Extraordinary men they were. Heroes and scoundrels, men of wealth and men with little or nothing, rapacious men seeking to despoil the Indians and saintly missionaries seeking to save them, learned men and those who could scarcely write their names, seekers of gold and Indian slaves and lost cities, mountaineers to scale the highest peaks, surveyors, engineers, hydrographers, cosmographers, naturalists, military personnel and even a former president of the United States, all were united by at least one common bond—they investigated the unknown continent, and their endeavors enlarged man's knowledge of an unknown land.

The discovery of the continent was essentially accidental, for its existence was totally unsuspected. Columbus had organized his third voyage in 1498 for the purpose of discovering the mainland which King João II of Portugal believed existed in the equatorial region, and which the Admiral assumed had to be part of Asia. Subsequent exploration in the years following neither confirmed nor denied this thesis, and J. H. Parry suggests that Amerigo Vespucci and even Ferdinand Magellan may have sailed at first without comprehending that this land mass—this *mundus novus*—was not a part of Asia but a separate continent. Vasco Núñez de Balboa's discovery of the "South Sea"—an ocean the extent of which he could not have imagined—stirred men to search for a strait so that this inconvenient land mass could be bypassed and Asia reached at last. Not until Magellan's discovery of the strait that bears his name and his subsequent voyage to the Philippines could all doubt concerning the continental nature of South America be set aside. It was certainly not an extension of Asia.

The continent ceased to be considered merely as an inconvenient barrier with the discovery and conquest of the rich Inca and Chibcha realms. Land expeditions penetrated deep into the

Introduction

interior in the search for gold and silver, while daring navigators explored the coastlines to reinforce the claims of Spain and Portugal, to map the region, and to determine with exactitude the precise location of the western entrance to the Strait of Magellan. Meanwhile, the Rio de la Plata system had been explored in the search for silver and the realm of the "White King," and as a result of Gonzalo Pizarro's futile quest for cinnamon, Francisco de Orellana made the first journey down the Amazon River. What is more remarkable about all this is the rapidity of it. Within little more than half a century after Columbus' discovery, the coasts of South America had been mapped with a surprising degree of accuracy, the interior had been penetrated from several directions, and the continent had been crossed in that memorable journey down the Amazon. Yet North America was still being depicted as an extension of Asia, and its outline would not be mapped as accurately for centuries to come.

The seventeenth century was a period of expansion. From the settled life of the cities, missionaries advanced into the interior to make converts of the Indians and produced the first maps of this hitherto unexplored territory. In Brazil, the *bandeirantes* pushed into the backlands in search of Indians to capture for the slave market, and for gold and diamonds once their presence became known. Several parties penetrated into the heart of the continent—the first explorers to do so. And it was during this period, through the efforts of Portuguese explorers and missionaries, that Portugal was able to lay claim to and occupy the Amazon valley. The discovery of riches in the interior of Brazil led to the opening of new access routes and the first mapping of many areas. The refusal of other European powers to accept a world dividend between Spain and Portugal led to attempts by France to enter the southern part of the continent, and to a Dutch search for a new passage to the South Sea and India which led to the discovery of Cape Horn and the realization that Tierra del Fuego, almost universally believed to be a part of a vast southern continent, was in reality an island. Meanwhile, several expeditions searched in vain for "the enchanted city of the Caesars" in the southern Andes but did discover the beautiful lakes in that area. Not until the end of the eighteenth century did the last expedition set out on this useless enterprise.

Foreign exploration continued in the eighteenth century, as

British and French navigators explored extensively the coasts of Patagonia and the west coast of the continent, resulting in the foundation of new Spanish settlements so that the area would not be lost to Spain. But this century is memorable most of all for the beginning of extensive scientific exploration. A French expedition seeking to take measurements at the equator to aid in determining whether or not the earth was a perfect sphere resulted in an extensive survey of the region around Quito and the exploration of the Amazon valley by these scientists on their return journey. Other scientific expeditions by sea had begun early in the century but were interrupted by the series of colonial wars; not until later in the century could Captain James Cook and especially the Spanish expedition under Alejandro Malaspina carry out their extensive scientific reconnaissance. On the continent, botanists busied themselves collecting new and unusual specimens, many destined for the royal botanical gardens in Madrid. Longstanding boundary disputes between Spain and Portugal were finally settled by the Treaty of San Ildefonso in 1777, and boundary commissions began the long and arduous task of surveying the limits agreed upon. As a result, accurate maps of many areas were produced for the first time.

By the beginning of the nineteenth century, the exploration of the continent, in the ordinary sense of the term, was nearing completion. The major rivers, mountains, deserts, forests, and plains had given up their secrets, and few areas remained where civilized man had not yet trod. The journey of Alexander von Humboldt and Aimé Bonpland to South America brought about a change of direction and purpose; scientific investigation was to be the dominant theme of the century, and naturalists would be the leading explorers. The natural history of the continent was subsequently studied by numerous government and privately sponsored expeditions. Hydrographic, geological, and geodesic studies were made, the deserts were investigated, and the highest mountains scaled. The role of the explorer at that time, as the Swiss-American naturalist Louis Agassiz remarked, was to investigate not to discover. It was a period of intense activity, and resulted in a great expansion of knowledge.

Scientific activity continued in the twentieth century, but there were other investigations of a different nature. In a search for the last Inca stronghold, Hiram Bingham came upon the lost

Introduction

city of Machu Picchu, perhaps unwittingly rekindling interest in lost cities which seemed to have died out at the end of the eighteenth century; P. H. Fawcett later lost his life in a futile search for a lost city in the interior of Brazil. Earlier, Theodore Roosevelt had ruined his health in exploring the mysterious "River of Doubt." But the greater part of recent exploration has been less romantic and spectacular. The search for oil and ore, the study of remote Indian tribes still living in much the same way as they had at the time of the discovery, efforts to improve communications by the construction of landing strips, railroads, and highways, the building of new cities in the interior, and detailed air surveys have eliminated nearly all *terrae incognitae* from the map.

The arrangement of materials in this bibliography follows a topical pattern. First place is given to general bibliographical guides which contain sections dealing with the exploration of South America, with specific aspects of it, or specific personalities involved in it. Following are various collections of printed documents, both those general in nature and those dealing specifically with certain geographical areas or voyages. Next appear various collections of narratives of voyages of discovery and exploration, which appear alphabetically by author or editor of the collection.

A combined chronological and topical organizational scheme is used for the remainder of the bibliography. Under each heading and sub-heading, primary source materials appear first, followed by secondary. The initial listings are general histories of discovery and exploration, followed by works on geography and cartography of special interest for this specific field. For general historical information on South America, sections on general histories of the Indies and histories of specific areas are included. These are followed by a section on myths and legends, since such fables as El Dorado, the Enchanted City of the Caesars, the White King, and Lake Parima and the "golden city of Manoa" were powerful motivating forces in exploration. The remaining divisions are chronological by centuries, with topical subdivisions. Author and topical indexes are provided which will quickly direct the researcher to the appropriate section and should make the location of desired sources, both primary and secondary, relatively easy.

It is obvious, of course, that a work of this nature cannot

include every book or article concerned with the discovery and exploration of South America. The literature on such towering figures as Columbus and Magellan, for example, would easily fill very many pages, and to attempt to list them all would not only greatly overburden the bibliography under those headings but would also be somewhat unnecessary in view of the existence of adequate bibliographies. I have chosen to list, in such instances as these, only the most significant works, and to include those specialized bibliographies to which a researcher with specific interest in a restricted area might divert his attention. Where no such specific bibliographies exist, as, for example, in the case of Alexander von Humboldt, I have expanded the entries to make up in part for this deficiency. I have annotated all entries which I have either seen myself or for which I have an adequate appraisal, with the exception of such titles as do not appear to require comment.

The publication of this bibliographical guide indicates the wealth of material already available to scholars and to others interested in the exploration of South America. The extensive collections of voyages, the personal and official accounts of voyages, the valuable printed collections of documents, and the great number of secondary sources, most of which are of high quality, provide an extensive array of source materials and a firm basis for further study. Yet it is obvious that despite all that has been done, there is a need for further scholarly productivity in almost every specific area of this field of study. Specialized bibliographies would be highly desirable for such fields as, for example, the exploration of the Andes, the great river systems, and specific geographical areas; they are needed also for such fields as missionary exploration and scientific exploration. The latter need will eventually be met in part by Professor Robert Ryal Miller's "Checklist of Naturalists in Latin America in the Nineteenth Century," now in progress. The need for an updating of bibliographical resources is being met by Barbara B. McCorkle's articles "Recent Literature in Discovery History" in *Terrae Incognitae*.

The continued publication of the explorer's own narratives should be accorded high priority. There are no recent counterparts of such collections as those of John Callander, Anshawn

Churchill, Edwin Cavendish Drake, Richard Hakluyt, Robert Kerr, Martin Fernandez de Navarrete, and Samuel Purchas, although the Hakluyt Society has published several hundred accounts in its regular and special series, and the *Biblioteca de autores españoles* numbers many narratives of the Spanish explorers among its volumes. Such specialized collections as Pedro de Angelis' documents and works on Argentine history, Juan Friede's on Colombian history, Affonso de Escragnolle Taunay's documents on the "monsoons" (expeditions into the interior of Brazil), and the various collections of letters and documents from the Jesuit missions might, it is to be hoped, inspire the publication of similar collections for other areas of study.

There is also a need to fill in many of the great gaps existing in narrative history. There is, for example, aside from Richard B. Morse's admirable collection of selections from outstanding authorities and an English translation of Vianna Moog's study, both single-volume works, no extensive treatment of the *bandeirantes* in English, despite the wealth of material available. Nor is there a comprehensive study of the missionaries as explorers. The expedition of Charles-Marie de La Condamine still awaits its historian, as does that of Malaspina and the other great eighteenth-century scientific explorers, although the recent appearance of Iris Engstrand's study does much to fill that void. Much of great value and interest can be done in the field of scientific exploration as the works of Arthur Steele, Robert Ryal Miller, and Lewis McKinney demonstrate. There is no biography of José Celestino Mutis nor any significant appraisal of his work in English, although he accumulated one of the largest herbariums in the world in Bogotá. There is no study in English of the French botanist Auguste de Saint-Hilaire, and only two volumes of Johann Baptist von Spix' and C. F. Martius' *Travels in Brazil in the Years 1817–20* have been translated from the German. Karl Ferdinand Appun's *Unter den Tropen* appears in a Spanish translation, but not in English. Obviously not every explorer's account of his travels can or needs to be translated, but the major ones are certainly deserving of it.

Good histories are needed which will cover various aspects of exploration in South America in the nineteenth and twentieth centuries. For the most part, the only available sources are the narratives written by the explorers themselves, which necessarily leave each expedition isolated. Here is a rich field indeed for further study. Biographical studies are extremely important, yet biographers have generally limited themselves to the great discoverers and explorers of the early period; only a few of the great naturalists of the nineteenth century have been accorded a similar honor. And yet, the nineteenth century, as well as our own, have produced a considerable number of explorers whose lives and exploits would make excellent subjects for biographies. Perhaps too, in the future, we might hope to see the re-issuing of the first-hand narratives of some of the great explorers of these last two centuries, edited and annotated in the format of the Hakluyt Society's publications.

There remains a note of acknowledgment. I would like first of all to express my appreciation to my one-time colleague at the University of Illinois, Professor Charles E. Nowell, for the great interest he took in my *The Explorers of South America* and for his valuable suggestions on source materials, which are incorporated in this volume, and to Professor John Thompson of the Department of Geography of that university, who first encouraged me to publish this bibliography. To Mr. Oliver Dunn, former associate director of libraries at Purdue University and to Professor Robert Ryal Miller, formerly of California State University at Hayward, I am indebted for many valuable suggestions. I much appreciate the assistance of Dr. John Hébert, Deputy Chief of the Hispanic Foundation of the Library of Congress, for his generous assistance in tracking down some elusive information. And finally, I owe much to Professor James A. Casada of the Department of History and Geography at Winthrop College for his valuable advice and assistance as editor of this series.

Edward J. Goodman

Cincinnati, Ohio
November 12, 1981

The Exploration of South America

I. BIBLIOGRAPHICAL GUIDES

1. American Historical Association. *Guide to Historical Literature.*

2. Anderson, Yeatman III. *From Columbus to Mackenzie, 1492 to 1801. Check List of Books Relating to the Discovery and Exploration of America.* Cincinnati: Public Library of Cincinnati and Hamilton County, 1961.

   An annotated list of 196 books, many of them relating to the exploration of South America, in the Rare Book Department of the Public Library of Cincinnati and Hamilton County at the time of publication.

3. Ballester y Castell, Rafael. *Las fuentes narrativas de la historia de España durante la edad moderna, 1478-1808.* Fascicula primero. Los reyes católicos. Carlos I. Felipe II. Valladolid, 1927.

4. Berger, Paulo. *Bibliografia do Rio de Janeiro de viajantes e autores estrangeiros, 1531-1900.* Rio de Janeiro: São José, 1964.

   Despite its title, this bibliography is not restricted to libraries in Rio de Janeiro.

5. Burns, E. Bradford. "A Working Bibliography for the Study of Brazilian History." *The Americas*, 22 (July 1965): 54-88.

5a. Dutcher, George M., et al., eds. *A Guide to Historical Literature.* New York: Macmillan, 1931.

6. Ganzemuller de Blay, Maria Luisa. *Contribucion a la bibliografia viajera y descriptiva de Venezeula: coleccion de 467 fichas.* Caracas: Escuela de Biblioteconomia y Archivos, 1964.

   A valuable, well-annotated list of 467 narratives of exploration and travel in Venezuela.

7. Giraldo Jaramillo, Gabriel. *Bibliografía colombiana de viajes*. Bogotá: Editorial ABC, 1957.

    This list of some 300 titles is concerned chiefly with travel in the nineteenth century.

8. Griffin, Charles C., ed. *Latin America: A Guide to the Historical Literature*. Austin: University of Texas Press, 1971.

9. Gropp, Arthur E. *A Bibliography of Latin American Bibliographies*. Metuchen, N.J.: Scarecrow Press, 1968. Supplement, 1971.

    The author was librarian of the Columbus Memorial Library in Washington. This is an updating of the second edition (1942) compiled by C.V. Jones.

10. ------. *A Bibliography of Latin American Bibliographies Published in Periodicals*. 2 vols. Metuchen, N.J.: Scarecrow Press, 1976.

    There are no specific sections on discovery and exploration. The section on maps (Vol. 2:728-32) contains some useful items.

11. Moraes, Rubens Borba de, and William Berrian, eds. *Manual bibliográfico de estudos brasileiros*. Rio de Janeiro: Gráfica Editora Souza, 1949.

    The most extensive and complete bibliography on Brazilian history: It contains items published through 1945.

12. Rodrigues, José Honório. *Historiografía del Brasil, Siglo XVI*. México, D.F.: Instituto Panamericano de Geografía e Historia, 1957.

    A shorter (102 pp.) but valuable work listing the most important works of a number of outstanding historians.

13. Torodash, Martin. "Columbus Historiography Since 1939." *Hispanic American Historical Review*, 46 (Nov. 1966): 409-28.

14. ------. "Magellan Historiography." *Hispanic American Historical Review*, 51 (May 1971):313-35).

II. COLLECTION OF DOCUMENTS

15. Berchet, Guglielmo. *Fonti italiane per la storia scopters del Nuovo Mondo.* 2 vols. Roma: Ministero della Pubblica Instruzione, 1892-93.

    The set contains illustrations and facsimiles. Vol. 1 is devoted to diplomatic correspondence, vol. 2 to other documents.

16. Chelho, José, et al. *Alguns documentos do Archivo da Torre do Tombo, acerca das navigacõ e conquistas portuguezas publicados por ordem do governo de sua majestade fidelissima as celebrar-se a commemorão quadricentenaria do descobrimento da America.* Lisboa, 1892.

    A careful selection of documents on discovery and conquest from 1416 to 1554.

17. Comitato onoranze ad Amerigo Vespucci nel quinto contenario della nascita. *Raccolta di carte e documenti esposti alla Mostra tenuta in Palazzo Vecchio a Firenze nel V. Centenario della nascita di Amerigo Vespucci.* Firenze, 1955.

    A folio volume of 34 plates, with no text. It contains some excellent maps.

18. Cortesão, Jaime, ed. "*Documentos para a historia da conquista e colonização de leste-oeste do Brasil.*" *Anais da Bibliotheca Nacional do Rio de Jeneiro.* 26 (1905): 150-526.

19. Friede, Juan. *Documentos inéditos para la historia de Colombia.* 10 vols. Bogotá: Academia Colombiana de Historia, 1955-60.

    A collection of documents from 1509-1550 from the Archivo General de Indias in Seveille. Indexed.

20. Garay, Blas. *Colección de documentos relativos a la historia de América y particularmente a la historia del Paraguay.* Asunción: Talleres Nacionales de H. Kraus, 1899.

21. Harrisse, Henry. *Bibliotheca americana vetustissima. A Description of Works Relating to America Published Between the Years 1492 and 1551.* New York: G.P. Philes, 1866. Additions. Paris: Imp. W. Drugulin, 1872, Madrid: Librería General V. Suárez, 1958.

    Contains footnotes and facsimiles of rare items.

22. Italy, Reale Commissione Colombiana. *Raccolta di documenti e studi pubblicati della Reale Commissione Columbiana pel quarto centenario dalla scopterа dell' America.* 15 vols. Roma, 1892-94.

    A monumental work prepared to commemorate the four hundredth anniversary of the discovery of America. It contains the texts of important documents as well as a number of scholarly articles.

23. Malheiro Dias, Carlos, ed. *História de colonizacão porquêsa do Brasil.* 3 vols. Pôrto: Litografia Nacional. 1924.

    A collection of documents relating to the Portuguese colonization of Brazil.

24. Medina, José Toribio. *Colección de documentos inéditos para la historia de Chile, desde el viaje de Magallanes hasta la batalla de Miapó, 1518-1818.* 30 vols. Santiago de Chile: Imp. Ercilla, 1882-1902. Segunda serie, 3 vols. Santiago de Chile: Fondo Histórico y Bibliográfico J.T. Medina, 1956-59.

    A monumental collection by Chile's greatest historian. Vols. 1-8 of the first series are pertinent to the period of discovery and early exploration. The second series covers the period 1558-89. There is a general index to the first series; there is an index at the beginning of each volume of the second series.

25. ———. *El veneciano Sebastián Caboto al servicio de España y especialmente de su proyectado viaje a las Molucas por el Estrecho de Magallanes.* Tomo II. Documentos. Santiago de Chile: Impr. y Encuadernación

Universaria, 1908.

This is the most comprehensive collection on Sebastian Cabot and his voyage, printing every document known to exist.

26. Portugal. *Os sete únicos documentos de 1500, conservados em Lisboa, referentes à viagem de Pedro Alvares Cabral.* Lisboa: Agência geral das colónias, 1940.

    The printed texts, with photographs of the original documents and excellent notes and comments by the editors, Capt. Fontuora da Costa and Dr. António Baião.

27. Ramusio, Giovanni Battista. *Navigationi et viaggi.* Vol. 3. Venezia, 1559.

    This volume, last of three, contains documents on Colombus and several of the *conquistadores.*

28. Spain. *Colección de documentos inéditos para la historia de España.* 112 vols. Madrid, 1842 ff. Volume 5, 193-388 contains documents relative to the conquest of Peru.

29. ———. *Documentos inéditos para la historia de España.* Publicados por los señores Duque de Alba, Duque de Maura, Conde de Gamazo, Conde de Heredia-Spínola, Marqués de Aledo, Marqués de Vega de Anzo Duque de Fernán-Núñez. Madrid: Tip. de Archivos, 1936- .

    Vols. 1 and 2 have material on Walter Raleigh. Vol. 8 contains the Bulls of Demarcation of Pope Alexander VI and the Treaty of Tordesillas. Vols. 9-12 contain the *Epistolario* of Peter Martyr.

30. Spain. Ministerio de Fomento. *Cartas de Indias.* Publicadas por primera vez el Ministerio de fomento. Madrid: Imp. de M.G. Hernández, 1877.

    A collection of 108 letters from civil and religious authorities in the Indies, covering the years 1496-1586, with notes and maps.

31. ———. Ministro de Ultramar. *Colección de documentos inéditos relativos al descubrimiento, conquista,*

y colonización de las posesiones españoles en
América y Occidental. 1ª ser. 42 vols. 2ª ser.
22 vols. Madrid, 1895-1922.

Documents, chiefly from the sixteenth century, selected from the vast collection in the Archivo General de Indias in Seville by Juan Bautista Muñoz. There are some inaccuracies in transcription, but the collection has the distinct advantage of availability.

32. Urteaga, Horacio H., and Carlos A. Romero, eds. *Colección de libros y documentos referentes a la historia del Perú.* 12 vols. Lima, 1916-19.

III. COLLECTIONS OF CONTEMPORARY ACCOUNTS

33. Angelis, Pedro de. *Colección de obras y documentos relativos a la historia antigua y moderna de las provincias del Río de la Plata.* 6 vols. Buenos Aires: Imprenta del Estado, 1837.

    A good and valuable collection of contemporary accounts. Vol. 5, *Colección de viages y expediciones a los campos de Buenos-Aires*, contains much information on many little-known expeditions.

34. Barcia Carballido y Zuñiga, Andrés González de. *Historiadores primitivos de las Indias Occidentales.* 3 vols. Madrid, 1749.

    A valuable collection of the works of the earliest historians of the Indies. The rarest parts are the "Cartas de Cortés" and the *examen* of the narrative of Cabeza de Vaca in Vol. 1.

35. Callander, John, ed. *Terra Australis Cognita, or Voyages to the Terra Australis, or Southern Hemisphere during the Sixteenth, Seventeenth, and Eighteenth Centuries.* 3 vols. Edinburgh, 1746-48.

    An excellent collection comprising 37 major voyages to the southern hemisphere from Vespucci to Byron. Vol. 3 was edited by Charles de Brosses.

36. Churchill, Awnsham. *A Collection of Voyages and Travels, Some Now First Printed from Original MSS., Others Now First Published in England.* 3rd ed., 6 vols. London: Lintot and Osborn, 1744.

    An excellent collection of great utility.

37. *Colección de libros raros o curiosos que tratan de América.* 10 vols. Madrid, 1892.

A collection of various important books of considerable interest to the historian of discovery and exploration. Vols. 5-6 (bound together), for example, contain the *Historia del Almirante Don Cristóbal Colón ... por Don Fernando Colón, su hijo.*

38. Drake, Edward Cavendish. *A New Universal Collection of Authentic and Entertaining Voyages and Travels, from the Earliest Accounts to the Present Time.* London: J. Cooke, 1768.

    A brief but useful collection, similar to Churchill's *Collection* (No. 36).

39. Grynaeus, Simon. *Novus Orbis Regionum Ac Insularum Veteribus Incognitarum una cum Tabula Cosmographica.* Basel: Io Harvagium, 1555.

    Contains the first three voyages of Columbus, the voyages of Niño, Pinzón, Vespucci, and Cabral, as well as part of the fourth decade of Peter Martyr.

40. Hakluyt, Richard, ed. *The Principall Navigations, Voyages, Traffiques and Discoveries of the English Nation.* 12 vols. Glasgow: James MacLehose & Sons, 1904.

    The classic collection, first published in 1589. English translations of several Spanish and Portuguese accounts are included.

41. Herrera y Tordesillas, Antonio de. *Historia general de los hechos de los castellanos en las islas y tierra firme del mar océano (Décadas).* 9 parts in 4 vols. Madrid: Emplenta real, 1601-05. Madrid: Tipográfica de Archivos, 1934-57.

    A collection of accounts by contemporaries. An English translation by Capt. John Stevens (*The General History of the Vast Continents and Islands of America, Commonly Called the West Indies* ... London: J. Batley) appeared in 1725-26.

42. Kerr, Robert, ed. *A General History and Collection of Voyages and Travels, Arranged in Systematic Order* 17 vols. Edinburgh: Wm. Blackwood, and London: T. Cadell, 1824.

Vols. 3-5 and 10 pertain to South America. The collection is similar to that of Churchill (Item 36) but is far more extensive. It contains lengthy accounts of some of the early voyages and discoveries.

43. Navarrete, Martín Fernández de, ed. *Colección de los viajes y descubrimientos que hicieron por mar los españoles desdel fin del siglo XV, con varios documentos inéditos concernientes a la historia de la marina castellana y de los establecimientos españoles en Indias.* 5 vols. Madrid: Imprenta Real, 1829-59. Republished in Buenos Aires, 1945-46, and also appears as vols. 75-77 of the *Biblioteca de Autores Españoles*, Madrid: Ediciones Atlas, 1954-55.

    A superb collection of the most important works on sixteenth-century Spanish discovery and exploration.

44. Pinkerton, John, ed. *A General Collection of the Best and Most Interesting Voyages and Travels in All Parts of the World, Many of Which Are Now First Translated into English.* 17 vols. London: Longman, Hurst, Rees & Orne, 1808-14.

    A superb collection, one of the best in English. Vol. 14 contains Betagh on Peru, Ovalle on Chile, Bouguer's voyage to Peru, La Condamine, Ulloa, and Nieuhoff's travels in Brazil.

45. Prévost, Antoine Francois, ed. *Histoire générale des voyages ou nouvelle collection de touts les relations de voyages par mer et par terre.* 25 vols. La Haye: Pierre de Hout, 1747-80.

    An outstanding collection, beginning with Plato and ending with eighteenth-century exploration. Vol. 18 (1743) includes the discovery of America and the first two decades of the sixteenth century, vol. 19 (Amsterdam, 1772) includes Magellan's voyage and the conquest of Peru. Vol. 20 (Amsterdam, 1773) covers the exploration of the Amazon R. from the sixteenth to the eighteenth century, the exploration of the Río de la Plata in the sixteenth century, the Jesuit explorers, the Malvinas (Falkland) Is., and the Strait of Magellan. Vol. 21 embraces the exploration of the northern part of South America.

46. Purchas, Samuel. *Hakluytus Posthumus, or Purchase His Pilgrimes.* 20 vols. Glasgow: J. MacLehose & Sons, 1905-07.

   A continuation of Hakluyt (Item 40) from his notes and other sources, also containing works translated from Spanish and Portuguese. Like the former, an invaluable collection.

47. Ternaux-Compans, Henri. *Voyages, Relations et Mémoires originaux pour servir à l'histoire de la découverte de l'Amérique.* 20 vols. Paris: Bertrand, 1837.

   The first seven volumes contain material relating to the exploration of South America, some of it hitherto unpublished. There are some inaccuracies.

48. *Voyages and Discoveries in South America.* London: S. Buckley, 1698.

   A small, brief volume containing several valuable accounts published in their entirety.

IV. GENERAL BACKGROUND

A. Exploration in general.

49. Albion, Robert G., ed. *Exploration and Discovery*.
    New York: Macmillan Co., 1965.

    A brief, useful collection of articles on exploration from ancient times to the present. A good introduction to the subject.

50. Baião, António, Hernâni Cidade and Manuel Múrias, eds.
    História da expansão portuguêsa no mundo. 3 vols.
    Lisboa: Editorial Atica, 1940.

    A collaborative venture containing many excellent accounts of Portuguese discoveries and expansion. There are many superb illustrations and maps.

51. Baker, John N.L. A *History of Geographical Discovery and Exploration*. New ed. rev. New York: Cooper Square Publishers, Inc., 1967.

    This is the latest edition of this excellent, thoroughly sound survey. Chapters 5-7 refer to South America.

52. Beaglehole, John C. *The Exploration of the Pacific*.
    London: A.C. Black Ltd., 1934.

    An excellent survey of exploration from Ferdinand Magellan to Captain James Cook.

53. Boxer, Charles R. *Four Centuries of Portuguese Expansion, 1415-1825; a Succinct Survey*. Johannesburg; Witwatersrand University Press, 1961.

    A very brief survey. Chapter 4 is concerned with the discovery and settlement of Brazil.

54. Brownell, Henry Howard. *The Discoverers, Pioneers, and Settlers of North and South America.* Boston: H. Wentworth, 1853.

    The first half of this book, which is based on original sources, covers the period of discovery and conquest.

55. Burney, James. *A Chronological History of the Discoveries in the South Sea or Pacific Ocean.* 5 vols. London: L. Hansard, 1803-17.

    Contains numerous illustrations, plates, and maps.

56. Cortesão, Jaime. *Os descobrimentos portuguêses.* 2 vols. Lisboa: Editória Arcádia, 1962.

    An excellent work by one of Portugal's leading historians, with superb illustrations and maps. both contemporary and recent.

57. Dainelli, Giotto. *La conquista della terra. Storia delle esplorazioni.* Torino, 1950.

    A good, accurate survey of the subject. Pp. 211-305 are pertinent to Latin America.

58. Dantín Cereceda, Juan, ed. *Exploradores y conquistadores de Indias. Relatos geográficos.* Madrid: Instituto-escuela, 1934.

    A survey of geographical explorations from 1492 to 1540.

59. Figuerdo, Fidelino de. "The Geographical Discoveries and Conquests of the Portuguese." *Hispanic American Historical Review,* 6 (Feb.-Aug. 1926):47-70.

    Covers social conditions in Portugal, ship construction, cartography, nautical astronomy, and economic development.

60. Friederici, Georg. *Der Charakter der Entdeckung und Eroberung Amerikas durch die Europäer.* 3 vols., Stuttgart, 1925-26.

General Background

Vol. 1 of this first-class work covers the Spanish conquest, Vol. 2 the Germans in Venezuela and the Portuguese in Brazil.

61. Frontaura Argandoña, Manuel. *Descubridores y exploradores de Bolivia.* (*Enciclopedia Boliviana*, No. 25.) La Paz-Cochabamba: Editorial "Los Amigos del Libro," 1971.

    An excellent, well-written account incorporating source materials, with maps and illustrations. The only work of its kind.

62. Galvão, Antônio. *The Discoveries of the World ... to 1555.* Ed. by Vice-Adm. Bethune. London: The Hakluyt Society, 1862.

    A good edition of this important work, which includes discoveries by Spain and Portugal.

63. Gillespie, James Edward. *A History of Geographical Discovery 1400-1800.* (Berkshire Studies.) New York: Holt, 1933.

    A good, brief introduction to the subject.

64. Goodman, Edward J. *The Explorers of South America.* New York: Macmillan Co., 1972.

    A survey of the exploration of South America from Christopher Columbus' discovery in 1498 to Col. P.H. Fawcett's search for a "lost city" in 1925, with maps and illustrations.

65. Hanson, Earl P. *South from the Spanish Main: South America Seen Through the Eyes of Its Discoverers.* New York: Delacorte Press, 1967.

    A good narrative of the exploits of the major discoverers and explorers, with extensive quotations from their writings, written by an explorer and geographer.

66. Heawood, Edward. *A History of Geographical Discovery in the Seventeenth and Eighteenth Centuries.* Cambridge: Cambridge University Press, 1912.

    An excellent, scholarly survey of this important period.

67. Johnson, William Henry. *The World's Discoverers*....
    Boston: Little, Brown, 1900.

    A useful volume containing a number of plates and maps.

68. Julien, Charles-André. *Les voyages de découverte et les premiers établissements (XVe-XVIe siècles)*.
    Paris: Presses Universitaires de France, 1948.

    An excellent, scholarly account, well-documented. It covers French discoveries from 1462 to c. 1750. Chs. 1 and 4 are pertinent to South America.

69. Lawrence, Arnold W., and Jean Young. *Narratives of the Discovery of America*. New York: Cape, 1931.

    A good collection, with illustrations and maps.

70. Le Gentil, Georges. *Découverte du monde*. Paris, 1954.

    A brief, excellent survey of the history of exploration from the earliest times to 1948.

71. Morison, Samuel Eliot. *The European Discovery of America. The Southern Voyages, 1492-1616*. New York: Oxford University Press, 1974.

    A comprehensive survey of the most important discoverers and explorers of the period. There are excellent maps, illustrations, and critical bibliographical notes. An interesting, scholarly work.

72. Nowell, Charles E. *The Great Discoveries and the First Colonial Empires*. Ithaca, N.Y.: Cornell University Press, 1954.

    A brief, valuable, scholarly survey.

73. Parias, Louis-Henri, et al., eds. *Histoire universelle des explorations*. 4 vols. Paris: Nouvelle Librairie de France, 1955-56.

    A very thorough work of sound scholarship, with numerous illustrations and maps.

General Background

74. Parry, John H. *The Age of Reconnaissance. Discovery, Exploration, and Settlement, 1450-1650.* Cleveland: World Publishing Co., 1963.

   Very useful on navigation, shipbuilding, and cartography. A work of excellent scholarship.

75. ———, *The Discovery of South America.* New York: Taplinger, 1979.

   An excellent work of high scholarship, with extensive quotations from the writings of the participants. It is profusely illustrated, and contains numerous reproductions of contemporary maps.

76. Penrose, Boies. *Travel and Discovery in the Renaissance, 1420-1620.* Cambridge, Mass.: Harvard University Press, 1952.

   An interesting, valuable, well-written book, especially useful on cartography of the period.

77. Peres, Damião. *História dos descobrimentos portugueses.* Pôrto: Portucalense Editora S.A.R.L., 1943.

   By an outstanding Portuguese historian; the best single-volume account. Chapters 14 and 15 deal with the Portuguese discovery and early exploration of Brazil.

78. Portugal. Ministério do Ultramar. *A Náutica dos descobrimentos.* 2 vols. Lisboa: Agência Geral do Ultramar, 1951.

   An excellent and useful collection of articles, conference proceedings, and unedited works of Admiral Gago Coutinho.

79. Stefansson, Vilhjalmur, and Olive R. Wilcox, eds. *Great Adventures and Explorations from the Earliest Times to the Present. As Told by the Explorers Themselves.* New York: Dial Press, 1947.

   An extensive collection of some value for South America.

80. Vives, Jaime Vicens. *Rumbos oceánicos: los navegantes hispanos.* Barcelona: Editorial Barna, S.A., 1946.

    A well-written, good secondary source.

81. Weise, Arthur James. *The Discoveries of America to the Year 1525.* New York: Putnam, 1884.

    A useful survey of the earlier discoveries and explorations, with maps and illustrations.

B. Geography and Cartography.

82. Alcedo, Antonio. *Diccionario geográficohistórico de las Indias Occidentales é América.* 5 vols. Madrid, 1786-89. Eng. trans. *The Geographical and Historical Dictionary of America and the West Indies.* 5 vols. London, 1812.

    The English edition is in some respects more useful, since it condenses the Spanish edition somewhat to make room for additional material, some from Alexander von Humboldt; it is enlarged to cover all of America rather than the restricted area of the original.

83. "Algunas aspectos de la Patagonia." *Revista Americana Geográfica,* 20 (Buenos Aires, August. 1943): 98-100.

84. Berwick, Jacobo María del Pilar Carlos Manuel Stuart Fitz-James, 10. Duque de. *Mapas españoles de América. Siglos XV-XVII.* Madrid, 1951.

    A folio-size volume containing a magnificent collection of maps.

85. Cortesão, Armando. *Cartografia e cartógrafos portugueses dos séculos XV e XVI.* (Contribuição para um estudo completo.) 2 vols. Lisboa: Edição da "Seara Nova," 1935. Vol. 2 contains reproductions of early maps. This valuable work has one flaw--an attempt to prove that Columbus was Portuguese.

86. ———, and Avelino Teixeira da Mota. *Portugaliae Monumenta Cartographica.* 6 vols. Lisboa, 1960-61.

General Background 19

These folio volumes contain reproductions of 1600 maps in 600 prints, some in color, printed to celebrate the fifth centenary of the death of Prince Henrique. There is also a historical text.

87. Enciso, Martin Fernandez de. *Suma de geografía.* Sevilla, 1579. Eng. trans. by Roger Barlow, London: The Hakluyt Society, 1931.

    The section on America is derived from Enciso's personal knowledge.

88. Humboldt, Alexander von. *Examen critique de l'histoire de la géographie du nouveau continent.* 5 vols. Paris: Gide, 1836-39.

    A monumental work by a great German scientist and naturalist, based in part on personal knowledge. It was long considered the authoritative work on the subject.

89. López de Velasco, Juan. *Geografía y descripción universal de las Indias.* Madrid, 1894.

    This work, written in 1571-74, is based on documents from the Consejo de Indias.

90. Puente y Olea, Manuel de la. *Estudios españoles. Los trabajos geográficos de la Casa de Contratación.* Sevilla, 1910.

91. Skelton, Raleigh A. *Explorers' Maps: Chapters in the Cartographic Record of Geographical Discovery.* New York: Praeger, 1958.

    A reprint with revisions of articles published in *The Geographical Magazine* (London) from 1953 to 1956. Well illustrated, with maps and charts.

92. Stevenson, Edward L. "Early Spanish Cartography of the New World, with Special Reference to the Wolfenbüttel-Spanish Map and the Work of Diego Ribero." *American Antiquarian Society Proceedings,* 19 (Worcester, Mass. 1909): 369-419. Also published separately. Worcester: Davis Press, 1909.

20   General Background

93. ———. " The Geographical Activities of the Casa de Contratación." *Annals of the Association of American Geographers,* Vol. 16 (1927).

94. ———. *Maps Illustrating Early Discovery and Exploration in America, 1502-1530.* New Brunswick, N.J., 1903.

   Photographic reproductions from original manuscripts.

95. Suárez de Figueroa, Lorenzo, ed. *Relaciones geográficas de Indias.* 3 vols. Lima, 1885.

   This work was originally written in 1586.

96. Vidal de la Blache, Paul M. *La Rivière Vincent Pinzon. Etude sur la cartographie de la Guayane.* Paris: Félix Alcan, 1902.

   A scholarly work by one of France's leading geographers.

97. Vindel, Francisco. *Mapas de America en los libros expañoles de los siglos XVI al XVIII (1503-1798).* Madrid, 1955.

98. Waldseemüller, Martin. *The "Cosmographiae Introductio" of Martin Waldseemüller in Facsimile. Followed by the Four Voyages of Amerigo Vespucci, with Their Translation into English, to Which Are Added Waldseemüller's Two World Maps of 1507.* Introduction by Joseph Fischer, S.J. and Franz von Wieser. Ed. by Charles G. Habermann. New York, 1907. Ann Arbor, Mich.: University Microfilms, 1966.

99. Wilgus, Alva Curtis. *Maps Relating to Latin America in Books and Periodicals.* Washington: Pan American Union, 1933.

C. General Histories of the Indies.

100. *An Account of the Spanish Settlements in America. In Four Parts....* Edinburgh: A. Donaldson & J. Reid for the author, 1762.

   A useful work, based on original sources.

General Background

101. Acosta, José de. *The Natural and Moral History of the Indies.* Reprinted from the Eng. trans. of Edward Grimston, 1604. Ed. with notes and introduction by Clements R. Markham. 2 vols. London: The Hakluyt Society, 1880. (The original text in Spanish, *Historia natural y moral de las Indias*, constitutes Vol. 73 of the *Biblioteca de Autores Españoles.*)

    An outstanding work on the history, anthropology, and natural history of the Indies by a noted sixteenth-century Jesuit scholar.

102. Ballesteros Gaibrois, Manuel. *Historia de América.* Madrid: Pegaso, 1946.

    A useful, well-written, brief account.

103. Benzoni, Girolamo. *La Historia del mondo nuovo, di M.G.B. Milanese. La qval tratta dell'isole & mari nuouamente ritrouati & delle nuoue Città da lui proprio vedute, per acqua & per terra in quattordeci anni.* Venetia: Francesco Rampazetto, 1565. English trans. *History of the New World.* London: The Hakluyt Society, 1857.

    The first book of travel in the New World.

104. Bourne, Edward Gaylord. *Spain in America 1450-1580.* New York: Harpers, 1904. (Republished in 1962 with an introduction and bibliographical supplement by Benjamin Keen.)

    Chapters 1 through 13 of this standard work deal with discovery and exploration.

105. Casas, Bartolomé de las. *Historia de las Indias.* 3 vols. México, D.F.: Biblioteca Americana, 1951. (The best Spanish edition. Also appears as Vols. 95-96 in *Biblioteca de Autores Españoles.* Madrid: Ediciones Atlas, 1957.)

    The Mexican publication is an excellent new edition of this classic. This highly controversial work is as much a polemic in favor of the Indians as it is history, but it contains much valuable information, and shows considerable insight into the implications

of the conquest. It is also available in a very
good, if abbreviated, English translation (*History
of the Indies*. Trans. and edited by Andree Collard.
New York: Harper & Row, 1971).

106. Cobo, Bernabé. *Historia del Nuevo Mundo*. 2 vols.
(*Biblioteca de Autores Españoles*, vols. 91-92.)
Madrid: Ediciones Atlas, 1958.

 This classic by a Jesuit missionary, which remained
 unpublished for 250 years, contains much information
 of value to the anthropologist and naturalist as
 well as to the historian.

107. Costa, Cândido. *As duas Américas*. 2nd ed. rev.
Lisboa: J. Bastos, 1900.

 This work is of some utility, but claims that the
 Portuguese discovered America and makes the startling
 assertion that the Amazon was found by ships sent out
 by King Solomon.

108. Cronau, Rudolf. *Amerika. Die Geschichte seiner
Entdeckung von ältesten bis auf die neuste Zeit.*
6 vols. Leipzig, 1892.

 An excellent, well-written survey. Vols. 1-2 deal
 with the discovery and the sixteenth-century explorers.

109. Lizárraga, Reginaldo. *La descripción y población de
las India*. Lima: Imp. Americana, 1908.

 An interesting account by a Dominican priest, based
 on his sojourn in Peru, 1555-99.

110. Muñoz, Juan Bautista. *The History of the New World*.
Vol. 1 trans., with notes. London: C.G. & J.
Robinson, 1797.

111. Oviedo y Valdes, Gonzalo Fernández de. *Historia
general y natural de las Indias*. 5 vols. (*Biblioteca de Autores Españoles*, vols. 117-121.) Madrid:
Ediciones Atlas, 1959.

 A most valuable work by a contemporary of the *conquistadores* who had spent many years in the Indies.
 Because of his close attention to the natural history

General Background

of America he has been termed "the first naturalist in the New World."

D. Histories of Specific Areas.

112. Ballesteros y Beretta, Antonio. *Historia de España*. 12 vols. Barcelona: Salvat Editorial, 1948.

    The most complete and extensive scholarly treatment.

113. Barros Arana, Diego. *Historia general de Chile*. 11 vols. 2nd ed. Santiago: Editorial Nascimente, 1937.

    By one of Chile's leading historians. Vols. 1-2, 4-5, and 7 are especially pertinent to the discovery and exploration of Chile down to the end of the eighteenth century.

114. ———. *Origines de Chile*. 2 vols. Santiago, Editorial Nascimente, 1934.

    There is a good section on exploration.

115. Buarque de Holanda, Sérgio, ed. *História geral da civilizacão brasileira*. Vols. 1- . São Paulo: Difusão Européia do Livro, 1963- .

    An outstanding collaborative history of Brazil, well-balanced between colonial and later periods. Individual articles are by Brazil's leading contemporary historians.

116. Caulin, Fray Antonio. *Historia corográfica, natural, y evangélica de la Nueva Andalucía*. (*Biblioteca de Autores Españoles*, Vol. 107.) Madrid: Ediciones Atlas, 1946.

    An early history of Venezuela, with attention to natural history, by a Franciscan friar.

117. Cawkell, M.B.R., D.H. Maling, and E.M. Cawkell. *The Falkland Islands*. London: Macmillan, 1960.

    The best book on the subject. Does not accept the claim of a Spanish title based on prior discovery.

118. Charlevoix, Pierre F.-X. *The History of Paraguay.* 2 vols. London: Lockyer David, 1769.

119. Cieza de León, Pedro. *The Incas of Pedro de Cieza de León.* Trans. by Harriet de Onís. Ed. with introduction and notes by Victor Wolfgang von Hagen. Norman: University of Oklahoma Press, 1959.

    A classic account by the historian of the conquest of Peru. Good maps and illustrations.

120. Cortesão, Jaime, and Pedro Calmón. *Brasil.* (Vol. 26 in Antonio Ballesteros y Beretta, *Historia de America.*) Barcelona: Salvat Editores S.A., 1956.

    An excellent history of Brazil, concentrating on the colonial period.

121. Encina, Francisco A. *Historia de Chile desde la prehistoria hasta 1891.* 10 vols. Santiago: Editorial Nascimento, 1940.

    A classic history of Chile, marred by an anti-Church bias. Vol. 1, 2ª parte, Chs. 1-8 are useful.

122. Góngora Marmolejo, Alonso de. *Historia de Chile desde su descubrimiento hasta el año de 1575.* (Vol. 131 in *Biblioteca de Autores Espanoles.*) Madrid: Ediciones Atlas, 1960.

    A valuable account by a contemporary of the conquest.

123. González Suárez, Federico. *Historia general da la republica del Ecuador.* 8 vols. Quito: Daniel Cadena A., 1931.

    A good, lengthy survey of Ecuadorian history. Vol. 2 is pertinent to the discovery and conquest.

124. Haskins, Caryl P. *The Amazon.* New York: Doubleday, 1943.

    A lively, popular history of exploration of the Amazon.

125. Henao, Jesús M., and G. Arrubla. *Historia de Colombia.* 2 vols. in 1. 6th ed. Bogotá, 1936. (Eng. trans.

General Background

by J. Fred Rippy. Chapel Hill: University of North Carolina Press, 1938.

A good, dependable survey; a work of competent scholarship.

126. Leite, Duarte. *Brasil*. Barcelona: Salvat, 1956.

    A well-documented, well-written, useful survey of Brazilian history.

127. Levene, Ricardo. *A History of Argentina*. Trans. by William Spence Robertson. Chapel Hill: University of North Carolina Press, 1947.

    A good, dependable single-volume history of Argentina by one of its leading historians.

128. López, Vicente. *Historia de la República Argentina. Su origen, su revolución y su desarollo político hasta 1852*. Nueva ed. 10 vols. Buenos Aires: Librería la Faculdad, de Juan Roldán, 1911.

    This multi-volume standard work is somewhat outdated, but is still useful.

129. Martinic Beros, Mateo. *Historia del Estrecho de Magallanes*. Santiago: Editorial Andres Bello, 1977.

    An excellent, comprehensive survey of the history of the Strait from its geological beginnings to the present, highlighting the great explorers and Chile's claim. By the former intendant of Magallanes.

130. Randier, Jean. *Men and Ships Around Cape Horn, 1616-1939*. Trans. by M.W.B. Sanderson. New York: David McKay Co., 1966.

    A lavishly-illustrated, well-written, extremely interesting account of the sailing ships that rounded the dangerous cape. It is based on reliable printed sources and personal reminiscences of surviving sailors who had made the journey.

131. Riesenberg, Felix. *Cape Horn: the Story of the Cape Horn Region, Including the Straits of Magellan, from the Days of the First Discoverers*. New York:

Dodd, Mead & Co., 1939.

Captain Riesenberg, a prolific writer on the sea, presents the exploits of the major explorers of this region in a carefully researched, well-written book of great value.

132. Sierra, Vicente D. *Historia de la Argentina*. Vols. 1- . Buenos Aires: Union de Editores Latinos, 1958- .

An excellent collaborative work, of considerable value to the historian of discovery and exploration.

133. Southey, Robert. *History of Brazil*. 3 vols. London, 1819.

For a long time, this was the standard history of Brazil in English. Although considerably outdated, it is still good on the colonial period, and contains much material of value for the history of exploration and discovery of Brazil.

134. Vargas Ugarte, Ruben. *Historia del Perú*. Vols. 1- . Lima: Librería y Imprenta Gil and Buenos Aires: López, 1949- .

The work of a Peruvian Jesuit, this is a well-written and useful comprehensive history of Peru.

135. Varnhagen, Francisco Adolfo de, Visconde de Pôrto Seguro. *Historia geral do Brasil antes de sua separacão e independência de Portugal*. 4^a ed. 5 vols. São Paulo: Cia. Melhoramentos de São Paulo, 1927.

A sound, reliable work; the standard history of colonial Brazil.

136. Zárate, Agustín de. *Historia del descubrimiento y conquista del Perú*. (*Biblioteca de Autores Españoles*, Vol. 26) Madrid: Ediciones Atlas, 1946. (Appears also in Vol. 3 of Item 34.)

Although not a participant in the conquest, Zárate, a royal official and an accomplished historian, interviewed those who had and produced an interesting and careful record of the discovery and conquest. There is a good abbreviated English translation by J.M. Cohen (*The Discovery and Conquest of Peru*. Baltimore: Penguin Books, 1968).

D. Myths and Legends.

137. Adams, Percy G. *Travelers and Travel Liars, 1660-1800*. Berkeley and Los Angeles: University of California Press, 1962.

    A well-written, very interesting book. The chapter on the Patagonian giants is definitive.

138. Alexander, Hartley Burr. *Latin American Mythology*. Boston: Marshall Jones Co., 1920.

    Provides a good background for the subject. There are extensive notes and a good bibliography.

139. Arciniegas, Germán. "Historia secreta de El Dorado." *Farol*, 29 (Oct.-Dec. 1967): 2-3.

140. Bandelier, Adolph F. *The Gilded Man*. New York: D. Appleton & Co., 1893.

    An account of the legend as well as the expedition of Pedro de Ursúa and the tale of the Amazons.

141. Bayle, Constantino, S.J. *El Dorado fantasma*. 2^a ed. Madrid: Consejo de la Hispanidad, 1943.

    A history of the legend, the frontiers of "el Dorado," the Quesada family, etc.

142. Estellé, Patricio, and Ricardo Couyoudmdjian. "La ciudad de los Césares: origin y evolución de una leyenda (1526-1880)." *Historia*, 7 (Santiago, 1967): 339-75, 8 (1968): 333-65.

143. Fernández de Castillejo, Federico. *La Ilusión en la conquista. Génesis de los mitos y leyendas americanas*. Buenos Aires: Editorial Atalaya, 1945.

144. Gandía, Enrique de. *La ciudad encantada de los Césares*. Buenos Aires: A. García Santos, 1933.
    The definitive account by a leading Argentine historian.

145. Goodman, Edward J. "The Search for the Mythical Lake Parima." *Terrae Incognitae*, 7 (1976): 23-30.

    The story of the mythical lake in northern Brazil which appeared on nearly every map of South America from the sixteenth century well into the nineteenth.

146. Latcham, Ricardo E. *La Leyenda de los Césares: su origen y su evolución*. Santiago: Imp. Cervantes, 1929. (Also appears in *Revista Chilena de Historia y Geografía* (1929): 193-294.

    A very interesting and useful account of the legend.

147. Magalhães, Basílio de. "A lenda de Sabarabuçú." Congresso do Mundo Português, *Publicações*, 10 (Lisboa, 1940): 57-66.

    Although brief, this is one of the few writings available on this subject.

148. Nowell, Charles E. "Aleixo Garcia and the White King." *Hispanic American Historical Review*, 26 (Nov. 1946): 450-66.

    An excellent essay on the first European to reach the Inca realm. The best on the subject.

149. Shields, Robert Hale. "The Enchanted City of the Caesars, Eldorado of Southern South America." *Greater America: Essays in Honor of Herbert Eugene Bolton*. Berkeley and Los Angeles: University of California Press, 1945, pp-319-340.

    A very fine account, with a comprehensive bibliography.

V. FIFTEENTH- AND SIXTEENTH-CENTURY EXPLORATION

A. Early discoveries and exploration.

1. Primary sources.

150. Amat di San Filippo, Pietro. "Due lettere inedite di venturieri italiani in America (1534)." *Bolletino della Società geografica Italiana.* 22 (1885) 548-58.

The first letter, dated Dec. 24, 1534, is from Cosimo (? The letter is signed Tomaso F.) Fiaschi, a Florentine, who was with Welser and Alfinger in Venezuela. It is valuable for description. The second letter, which is anonymous (it may have been written by Genovese) is brief, and of less interest.

151. Anghiera, Pietro Martiro d'. *The Decades of the Newe World, or West India.* English trans. by Richard Eden. London: 1555.

The work of an Italian chaplain at the court of Queen Isabel I of Castile, based on his extensive correspondence and his interviews with returning explorers. The series of eight "Decades" was published under the title *De orbe novo* in 1530 at Alcalá. A more recent English translation under this title was made by F.A. MacNutt and was published in New York in 1912. The best edition is a Spanish translation by Jaoquín Torres Ascensio published in Buenos Aires in 1944 as Anglería, Pedro Mártir de, *Décades del Nuevo Mundo.* Two excerpts (Decade III, lib. IIII, 1502, and Decade III, lib. VI, 1516) appear in the *Raccolta* (Item 22), Part III, Vol. 2: 26-38.

2. Secondary sources.

152. Alamgia, Roberto. *L'Opera del genio italiano all' estero. I Primi esploratori dell'America.* Roma: 1937.

The voyages of Columbus, Vespucci (credited with only two voyages), the Cabots, and Verrazzano.

153. Costa, Abel Fontoura de. *A marinharia dos descobrimentos.* 2ª ed. Lisboa: 1939.

    A study of navigational methods used by the Portuguese.

154. Forero Benavides, Abelardo. "Los cronistas del descubrimiento." *Boletín Cultural y Bibliográfico*, 8 (6) (1965): 831-40.

155. García Franco, Salvador. "Como navegaban los descubridores." *Boletín de la Real Sociedad Geográfica*, 84 (July-December 1948): 336-37.

    A brief discussion of Spanish navigational methods by a Spanish naval officer.

156. Langnas, Izaac A. *A Dictionary of Discoveries.* New York: 1959.

    A useful work, containing short biographical sketches of most of the maritime explorers of Latin America.

157. Menéndez, Raul. "Esquema del Descubrimiento de América del Sur." *Revista Geográfica Americana*, 16 (October 1941): 238-66.

158. Morison, Samuel Eliot. *Portuguese Voyages to America in the Fifteenth Century.* Cambridge, Mass.: Harvard University Press, 1940.

    The definitive study; it successfully challenges the Portuguese so-called "policy of secrecy." There are good illustrations and maps.

159. Parry, John H. *The Age of Reconnaissance. Discovery, Exploration, and Settlement, 1450-1650.* Cleveland: World Publishing Co., 1963.

    Contains much information on early shipbuilding, navigation, and maps. There are good illustrations and maps.

Fifteenth- and Sixteenth- Century Exploration

160. ———. *The Discovery of South America*. New York: Taplinger Publishing Co., 1979.

    A superb piece of scholarship, based on, and containing extensive excerpts from, the accounts of the discoverers and explorers themselves. Mexico is included as well. The story is taken into the 17th century. There is a wealth of contemporary illustrations and maps.

161. Pinheiro, J.C. Fernandes. "Os Predecessores de Colombo. João Cousin." *Revista Trimensal do Instituto Histórico, Geográfico e Ethnographico do Brasil*, 37 (Parte segundo, 1874): 71-77.

    A discussion of Paul Gaffarel's thesis that Cousin accompanied by Vincente Yáñez Pinzón, reached America before Columbus.

162. Souza, Thomaz Oscar Marcondes de. "A astronomia náutica na época dos descobrimentos marítimos." *Revista de História* (São Paulo), 20 (41) (Jan.-March 1960): 41-63.

    A study of celestial navigation in the age of discovery, by one of Brazil's most distinguished historians.

163. ———. *O Descobrimento da América e a suposta prioridade dos Portugueses (de acordo com a história e a cartografia americana vetustíssima)*. São Paulo: Editoria Brasilense, 1944.

    An evaluation of all claims for a possible pre-Columbian discovery of America and a discovery of Brazil before Vicente Yáñez Pinzón. No evidence exists, the author claims, for anyone before Columbus or Pinzón, although Pedro Alvarez Cabral is acclaimed as the effective discoverer of Brazil.

164. ———. "A política de sigilo dos monarcas portuguesas da época dos descobrimentos marítimos." *Revista de História* (São Paulo), 18 (29) (April-June 1958): 158-68.

    A dispassionate appraisal of the so-called "policy of secrecy" of the Portuguese monarchs.

165. Vigneras, Louis-André. *The Discovery of South America and the Andalusian Voyages*. Chicago: University of Chicago Press for The Newberry Library, 1976.

   An outstanding work, essential for an understanding of the period. The first section is devoted to Columbus' third voyage, the Cabot voyage, and the idea of discovery of a continent; the second section covers eleven subsequent voyages, with stress on such matters as financing and recruiting.

B. The great discoverers.

   1. Christopher Columbus.

      a. Primary sources.

166. Colombo, Cristofero. *The Journal of Christopher Columbus*. Ed. by Louis-André Vigneras, tr. by Cecil Jane, with an Appendix by R.A. Skelton. London: Anthony Blond, 1968.

   A very informative edition of the *Journal*, with useful interpretations and a valuable appendix.

167. ———. *Journals and Other Documents on the Life and Voyages of Christopher Columbus*. Tr. and ed. by Samuel Eliot Morison. New York: Heritage Press, 1963.

   An excellent edition, with valuable notes and interpretations by one of the leading authorities on Columbus.

168. ———. *Select Documents Illustrating the Four Voyages of Columbus*. Tr. and ed. by Cecil Jane. 2 vols. London: The Hakluyt Society, 1930 and 1933.

   The second volume contains Columbus' narrative of the third voyage (pp. 1-71) with both the Spanish text and English translation.

169. ———. *Select Letters of Christopher Columbus, with Other Original Documents, Relating to His Four Voyages to the New World*. Tr. and ed. by R.H. Major. London: The Hakluyt Society, 1847.

Contains the account of the third voyage and a letter from the Admiral to the nurse of the Infante Juan.

170. ———. *The Voyages of Christopher Columbus. Being the Journals of His First and Third, and the Letters Concerning His First and Last Voyages, to Which is Added the Account of His Second Voyage Written by Andres Bernaldez.* Tr. and ed. with notes by Cecil Jane. London: Argonaut Press, 1930. (Reprint Amsterdam: Nico Israel, 1971.)

171. Colón, Fernando. *Historia del Almirante Don Cristóbal Colón ... escrita por Don Fernando Colón, su hijo.* 2 vols. (Vols. 5-6, *Colección de libros raros ó curiosos que tratan de América.*) Madrid: 1892. Trans. into English by Benjamin Keen as *The Life of the Admiral Christopher Columbus, by His Son, Ferdinand.* New Brunswick, N.J.: Rutgers University Press, 1959.

172. Trevisano, Agnolo. *Copia de littere mandate per Anzolo Trevisan.* MS. 1502.

   The sole source for a possible discovery of South America on Columbus' second voyage, 1494. There being no supporting evidence whatsoever, the claim would appear to have no validity. Known as the "Sneyd-Thatcher MS.," it may be found in the Rare Books Division of the Library of Congress.

B. Secondary sources.

173. *The American Traveller....* London: J. Fuller, 1743.

   Although planned as an extensive work, this is the only volume published. The second part deals with the voyages of Columbus.

174. Ballesteros y Beretta, Antonio. *Cristóbal Colón y el descubrimiento de América.* 2 vols. (Vols. 4-5 in Ballesteros, ed., *Historia de América.*) Barcelona: Salvat Editorial, 1945.

   An excellent account, thoroughly documented and annotated, by one of Spain's leading historians. The second volume contains the third voyage.

175. Camacho Cano, Enrique. *América através de los siglos. Historia general de América desde los tiempos más remotos hasta nuestros días.* 3 vols. Barcelona: Martinez y Cia., 1892-93.

   This work covers only up to and including Columbus, whose voyages appear in vols. 2 and 3.

176. Carreras y Valls, Ricardo. *Catalunya, descobridora d' America; la pre-descoberta i els catalans Joan Cabot i Cristófol Colom.* Barcelona, Imprenta Altes, 1929.

   Of little value. Of interest chiefly as an attempt to prove that Columbus and Cabot were Catalans.

177. Davies, Arthur. "The 'Miraculous' Dicovery of South America by Columbus." *Geographical Review*, 44 (Oct. 1954): 573-82.

   Claims that Columbus, led by Pedro de Ledesma, who had been there with the Portuguese, started out for Brazil on his third voyage, but changed course on July 31 and arrived at Paria.

178. Gandía, Enrique de. "Cristóbal Colón, el descubrimiento de América y las últimas investigaciones históricas." *Revista Geográfica de América*, 26 (Buenos Aires, Set. 1946): 149-56.

   A summary of the most recent Columbus scholarship to date (1946) by one of Argentina's most distinguished historians.

179. Irving, Washington. *A History of the Life and Voyages of Christopher Columbus.* 4 vols. London: John Murray, 1828.

   Vol. 2, Book 10 of this well-known but dated work is pertinent. Based on Herrera, Navarrete, Fernando Colón, Charlevoix, and Peter Martyr.

180. Molinari, Diego Luis. *La empresa colombiana.* Buenos Aires: Imprenta de la Universidad, 1938.

Fifteenth- and Sixteenth-Century Exploration

One of the best biographies of Columbus, by a distinguished Argentine historian. Well-illustrated, with good maps.

181. Morison, Samuel Eliot. *Admiral of the Ocean Sea: a Life of Christopher Columbus*. 2 vols. Boston: Little, Brown & Co., 1942.

    An outstanding study of Columbus as a navigator, by one of the most eminent Columbus scholars. A definitive work.

182. Navarrete, Martín Fernández de. *Viajes de Cristóbal Colón*. Madrid: Calpe, 1922.

    An excellent study by the nineteenth-century Spanish naval captain and historian, based on his great collection of Columbian documents.

183. Nowell, Charles E. "Reservations Regarding the Historicity of the 1494 Discovery of South America." *Hispanic American Historical Review*, 22 (Feb. 1942): 205-10.

    Challenges the thesis of William Jerome Wilson (Item 184) on the grounds of insufficient evidence.

184. Wilson, William Jerome. "The Historicity of the 1494 Discovery of South America." *Hispanic American Historical Review*, 22 (Feb. 1942): 192-205.

    Based on the writings of Agnolo Trevisano (the "Sneyd-Thatcher MS." (Item 172), the sole source for this "discovery." See C.E. Nowell's appraisal, Item 183.

185. ———. "The Spanish Discovery of the South American Mainland." *Geographical Review*, 31 (Apr. 1941): 283-99.

    Based on the Trevisano narrative (Item 172), which appears in translation in the text. A map shows the route of the supposed voyage, which is described as a search for pearls.

2. Amerigo Vespucci.

    a. Primary sources.

186. Varnhagen, Francisco Adolpho de, Visconde de Pôrto Segunro. *Amérigo Vespucci. Son caractère, ses écrits (même les moins authentiques), sa vie et ses navigations, avec une carte indiquant les routes.* Lima: Imprenta du Mercurio, 1865.

   A very rare work, reproducing Vespucci's works page by page, line by line. Each letter is preceded by a bibliographical notice.

187. Vespucci, Amerigo. *Amerigo Vespucci's Account of His First Voyage. Letter of Amerigo Vespucci to Pier Soderini, Gonfalonier of the Republic of Florence.* Boston: Directors of the Old South work, 1896.

   A brief account of the voyage.

188. ———. *Amerigo Vespucci's Account of His Third Voyage. From His Letter to Pier Soderini, Gonfalonier of the Republic of Florence.* Boston: Directors of the Old South work, 1898.

   A brief account.

189. ———. *The First Four Voyages of Amerigo Vespucci, Reproduced in Facsimile, with a Translation, Introduction, Map, and a Facsimile of a Drawing by Stradanus.* London: Bernard Quantsch, 1893.

   A brief, valuable work.

190. ———. *The Letters of Amerigo Vespucci and Other Documents Illustrative of His Career.* Trans. with notes and introduction by Clements R. Markham. London: Hakluyt Society, 1894.

   Contains letters to Soderini and to Lorenzo de' Medici, along with evidence of Alonso de Ojeda on the 1499 voyage.

191. ———. *El nuevo mundo. Cartas relativas a sus viajes y descubrimientos. Textos en italiano, español, y inglés.* Estudio preliminar de Roberto Levillier. Buenos Aires: Editorial Nova, 1951.

   An invaluable work, part of an excellent "Biblioteca Americanista" collection.

192. ———. *The Voyages of Americus Vespucius to the New World.* Appears in Item 42, Vol.3, 342-82.

   b. Secondary Sources.

193. *Amerigo Vespucci nel V. Centenario della Nascita.* [Numero speziale della *Revista Geografica Italiana.*] Firenze: La Nuova Italia, 1954.

   Contains Roberto Almagia's essay, "Alcane considerazioni sulla 'questione vespucciana'" and Tomaz Oscar Marcondes de Souza's "Amerigo Vespucci e la scoptere del Brasile," as well as a good bibliography.

194. Arciniegas, Germán. *Amerigo and the New World: the Life and Times of Amerigo Vespucci.* Trans. by Harriet de Onis. New York: Alfred A. Knopf, 1955.

   Despite a few errors of fact, this is a good, popular biography, rich in description. Supports the four-voyage theory, including a possible fifth voyage.

195. ———. "Navarrete y Amerigo Vespucci." *Boletín de Historia y Antigüedades,* 49 (Bogotá, 1962): 445-62.

   Claims that Navarrete was unfair in his treatment of Vespucci. Includes two documents from the Florentine archives.

196. ———. "Vespucci, una vida mal-tratada." *Boletín de Historia y Antigüedades,* 46 (Bogotá, 1959): 12-36.

   A defense of Vespucci; challenges the interpretations of Navarrete, Las Casas, and Magnaghi.

197. Avezac-Macaye, Armand d'. *Les voyages de Améric Vespuce au compte de l'Espagne, et les mesures itinéraires employées par les marins espagnols et portugais des XVe et XVIe siècles....* Paris: Imprimerie de L. Martinet, 1858.

   Good on Spanish and Portuguese navigational methods.

198. Casal, Pedro S. *Américo Vespucio y las costas Argentinas y Uruguayas*. Buenos Aires, 1953.

   A brief but very valuable work, with good maps.

199. Davies, Arthur. "The 'First' Voyage of Amerigo Vespucci in 1497-98." *Geographical Journal*, 108 (Sept. 1952): 331-37.

   A well-written article proposing a satisfactory solution to the question of the authenticity of this voyage: it was the same voyage as the "second" in 1499.

200. Gandía, Enrique de. "Los viajes fracasados de Vespucci a Cattigara, Taprobana y Malaca." *Revista de História*, 100 (São Paulo, 1974): 87-116.

   States that Vespucci's letters show that he was intent, on his 1501-02 voyage, on reaching Sumatra and Malacca via the Strait of Cattigara, that he got as far as $52°$ S., failing in his objective but finding land which was most likely the Malvinas (Falkland) Islands.

201. Levillier, Roberto. *América la bien llamada*. 2 vols. Buenos Aires: Editorial Guillermo Kraft, 1948.

   A work of careful scholarship, based on a thorough study of early maps of America. Holds to the four-voyage theory, claiming that all four must be accepted or none. Believes that Vespucci was probably the first to realize that Columbus had discovered a new world.

202. Magnaghi, Alberto. *Amerigo Vespucci: studio critico, con speciale riguardo a una nuova valutazione delle fonti*. 2 vols. Roma, 1924.

   Accepts three of the Vespucci letters, supporting two voyages; believes the others to be false. A classic statement of the two-voyage thesis. A one-volume revised edition was published in 1926.

203. Nowell, Charles E. "Levillier: *América la bien llamada*." *Hispanic American Historical Review*,

30, (Nov. 1950): 450-66.

An excellent critical essay on this controversial book.

204. Pedrosa, Manuel Xavier de Vasconcellos. "Indícios da presencia de Américo Vespúccio em Cabo Frio." *Revista do Instituto Histórico e Geográfico Brasileiro*, 287 (abril-junho 1970): 395-438.

205. Pohl, Frederick J. *Amerigo Vespucci: Pilot Major.* New York: Columbia University Press, 1944.

An excellent critical biography. Accepts the two-voyage thesis, and believes that Vespucci discovered Brazil.

206. Seco, Carlos. " Algunos datos definitivos sobre el viaje Hojeda-Vespúcio." *Revista de Indias* (Madrid enero-marzo 1955): 89-107.

States that Ojeda was in command of the 1499 voyage, which Vespucci left to explore on his own.

207. Souza, Thomaz Oscar Marcondes de. "Amerigo Vespucci e a prioridade de descobrimento do Brasil." *Revista de História* (Sao Paulo, abril-junho 1954): 253-71.

Believes that Vespucci discovered Brazil on his first ("second" according to the four-voyage thesis) voyage. By one of Brazil's leading historians.

208. ―――. *Amerigo Vespucci e suas viagens. Estudo Crítico de acordo com a documentacão histórica e cartográfica.* São Paulo: Universidade de São Paulo, Boletim CV, 1949.

Adopts Magnaghi's two-voyage approach. Believes that Vespucci discovered Brazil and probably the Rio de la Plata. An excellent, competent presentation.

209. ―――. *Amerigo Vespucci e suas viagens.* São Paulo: Instituto Cultural Italo-brasileiro, 1954.

Essentially a revision of Item 208; defends the Magnaghi two-voyage thesis against Levillier. (Item 201)

210. ──────. " A expedição de 1500-02 e Américo Vespucci."
(Instituto Histórico e Geográfico Brasileiro, IV
Congresso de História Nacional, Abril 1949. Anais,
Quarto Volume, 145-66.) Rio de Janeiro: Depto. de
Imprenta Nacional, 1950.

Believes that this is the best-proved voyage. The
nomenclature of Canerio's map is the result of this
expedition.

3. Ferdinand Magellan.

a. Primary sources.

Albo, Francisco. "Diario o Derrotero del Viaje de
Magallanes." Navarrete, Martín Fernández de,
Colección de Viajes (Item 43) Vol. 4, 209-247.

211. Nowell, Charles E., ed. Magellan's Voyage Around the
World. Three Contemporary Accounts. Evanston, III.:
Northwestern University Press, 1962.

An excellent work, invaluable for any study of
Magellan. It contains Antonio Pigafetta's First
Voyage Around the World, Maximilian of Transylvania's
"Letter to the Cardinal Archbishop Lord of Salzburg,"
and an excerpt from Gaspar Corrêa's Lendas da India.

212. Pigafetta, Antonio. Il primo viaggio intorno al globo
di Antonio Pigafetta, Sue Regole sull'arte de
navigare, per Andrea da Moste. Roma: Auspice
il Ministero della Pubblica Istruzione, 1894.

The Italian text of Pigafetta's work; a good edition.

213. ──────. Relation du premier voyage autour du monde
par Magellan, 1519-1522. Commenté et transcrit d'
après le manuscrit français par Léonce Peillard.
Paris: Club des Libraires de France, 1956.

Contains notes and a bibliography. A lengthy,
excellent piece of scholarship, with maps and porto-
lani.

214. Stanley, Henry Edward John Thomas, Baron Alderly.
The First Voyage Around the World, by Magellan.
Translated from the accounts of Pigafetta and

Other Contemporary Writers. London: The Hakluyt Society, 1874.

This is No. 52 in the Society's First Series of publications. There are excellent maps, facsimilies, and plates.

b. Secondary sources.

215. Benson, Edward Frederic. *Ferdinand Magellan*. New York: Harpers, 1930.

A good popular account, based on Spanish sources but containing (as the author states) "no new material."

216. Davies, Arthur. " A navegacão de Fernão de Magalhães." *Revista de História,* 22 (45)(São Paulo, jan.-marzo 1961): 173-89.

Maintains that Magellan remained south of the equator before turning west to cross the Pacific Ocean.

217. Guillemard, Francis H.H. *The Life of Ferdinand Magellan and the First Circumnavigation of the Globe.* London: George Philip & Son, 1890.

Samuel Eliot Morison rates this book, by a Cambridge professor and geographical editor of the Cambridge University Press who had traveled over parts of the route, as one of the best lives of Magellan. It was the first in English, and is based on primary sources. Appendices contain genealogies, lists of the personnel of the fleet, and the names of those who returned.

218. Hildebrand, Arthur Sturges. *Magellan*. London: Jonathan Cape, Ltd., 1925.

A good biography, based on Pigafetta and other primary sources, and Guillemard.

219. Koelliker, Oscar. *Die Erste Umseglung der Erde durch Fernando de Magallanes und Juan Sebastian del Cano, 1519-1522.* Munchen und Leipzig: R. Piper & Co. Verlag, 1908.

A thorough study, containing 32 tables and charts.

220. Lagoa, João António de Mascarenhas Judice, Visconde de. *Fernão de Magalhães (a su vida e a sua viagem) com um estudo náutico do roteiro, pelo almirante J. Freitas Ribeiro.* Prefácio do Dr. António Baião. Lisboa: Seara Nova, 1938.

   Actually two volumes in one, this is probably the best biography of Magellan in Portuguese. Volume 2 is given entirely to the voyage. The nautical study by Admiral Freitas Robeiro is excellent; there is a fine bibliography and appendix of documents.

221. Medina, José Toribio. *El descubrimiento del Océano Pacífico. Vasco Núñez de Balboa. Fernando de Magallanes y sus compañeros.* 2 vols. Santiago de Chile: Imprente Universitaria y Imprenta Elzeviriana, 1920.

   Volume 2 of this excellent work by the eminent Chilean historian is devoted entirely to Magellan. A first-class study.

222. ———. *El portugués Esteban Gómez al servicio de España.* Santiago de Chile, Imprenta de Elzeviriana, 1908.

   A brief study, with documents, of the captain who deserted Magellan at the Strait, by Chile's leading historian.

223. Melón y Ruiz de Gordejuela, Amando. *Los Primeros Tiempos de la Colonización. Cuba y las Antillas. Magallanes y la Primera Vuelta al mundo.* Tomo VI of Antonio Ballesteros y Beretta, ed., *Historia de América.* Barcelona: Salvat Editores S.A., 1952.

   A very detailed and accurate account. The last half of the work is devoted to Magellan and Elcano.

224. Mitchell, Mairin. *Elcano: the First Circumnavigator.* London: Herder, 1958.

   The only life of Elcano in English.

225. Navarette, Martín Fernández de. *Viaje de Magallanes y de Sebastián de Elcano alrededor del mundo.* Buenos Aires: Emecé Editores, 1944.

    A reprint of this Spanish classic.

226. Parr, Charles McKew. *So Noble a Captain. The life and Times of Ferdinand Magellan.* New York: Crowell, 1953.

    A well-written biography, with a good list of sources and their locations in the preface. Somewhat fictionalized, leaving many questions unanswered.

227. Queiroz-Velloso, José Maria de. *Fernão de Magalhães, a vida e a viagem.* Lisboa, 1941.

    Of considerable value; contains some new information.

228. Roditi, Edouard. *Magellan of the Pacific.* New York: McGraw-Hill, 1972.

    A good biography; the author tries to recapture the age in which Magellan lived, and events in which he may have participated. Regrettable, he states, it must be based on sources all too sketchy.

229. Zweig, Stefan. *Conqueror of the Seas: the Story of Magellan.* New York, Viking Press, 1938.

    A good, readable, popular biography.

C. Early discoveries: by areas.

   1. Brazil.

      a. Primary sources.

230. Abud, Katia Maria. "O descobrimento do Brasil através dos textos. A 'carta' de Pero Vaz de Caminha, texto diplomático." *Revista de História,* 36 (73) (São Paulo, jan.-marzo 1968): 185-227; 36 (74) (avr.-jun. 1968) 403-15.

    Part of an excellent series of articles presenting the texts of the sources, with notes and comment. See also Items 232, 233, 234, and 236.

231. Caminha, Pedro Vaz de. *Carta a El Rei D. Manuel.*
    (Obras completas de Jaime Cortesão, Vol. 2.)
    Lisboa: Portugália Editôra, 1967.

    Cortesão's edition of the first account of Brazil,
    with notes and a good bibliography.

232. Carvalho, Joaquim Barrades de. "O descobrimiento do
    Brasil através dos textos. III. A 'carta' de
    Mestre João." *Revista de História,* 32 (71) (São
    Paulo, jul.-sct., 1967): 179-93.

    Part of an excellent series of articles presenting
    the texts of the sources, with notes and comment. See
    also Items 230, 233, 234, and 236.

233. ———. "O descobrimento do Brasil através dos
    textos. IV. *O Esmeraldo de situ orbis* de Duarte
    Pacheco Pereira. *Revista de História,* 37 (76) (São
    Paulo, oct.-dez. 1968): 383-400; 38 (77) (jan.-marzo,
    1969): 149-91; 38 (78) (abr.-jun., 1969) 425-66; 39
    (80) (oct.-dez. 1969): 397-413; 40 (81) (jan.-marzo,
    1970): 153-77; 40 (82) (abr.-jun., 1970): 399-450.

    Part of an excellent series of articles presenting
    the texts of the sources, with notes and comment. See
    also Items 230,232, 234, and 236.

234. ———. "O descobrimento do Brasil através dos textos."
    Revista de História, 32 (65) (São Paulo, jan.-marzo,
    1966): 197-208.

    Commentary on the sources, with a bibliography. Part
    of an excellent series of articles. See also Items
    230, 232, 233, and 236.

235. Cortesão, Jaime. *A carta de Pero Vaz de Caminha.*
    Rio de Janeiro: Edições Livros de Portugal Ltda.,
    1943.

    A scholarly study of the first report on Brazil.

236. Makino, Miyoko. "O descobrimento do Brasil através
    dos textos. II. A Relação do Pilôto Anônimo."
    Revista de História, 34 (69) (São Paulo, jan.-marzo
    1967): 179-86.

Part of an excellent series of articles presenting the texts of the sources, with notes and comment. See also Items 230, 232, 233, and 234.

237. Motta, A Teixeira de. "Novos documentos sôbre uma expedição de Gonçalo Coelho ao Brasil entre 1503 e 1505." *Revista do Instituto Histórico e Geográfico do Brasil*, 287 (abril-junho, 1970): 483-91. Lisboa: Junta de Investigações do Ultramar, 1969.

    Two documents confirming Coelho as commander of an expedition to Brazil, 1503-05.

238. Souza, Pero Lopes de. *Diário de navegação de Pero Lopes de Souza de 1530 a 1532*. 2 vols. Rio de Janeiro: Typographica Leuzinger, 1927.

    The complete account. A critique of it was published as *Diário.... Estudo crítico pelo commandante Eugênio de Castro*. Prefácio de João Capistrano de Abreu. 2^a ed. Rio de Janeiro: Comissão Brasileira dos Centenários Portugueses, 1940. Vol. 1 contains the commentary, with bibliographical notes; Vol. 2 contains documents and maps.

    b. Secondary Sources

239. Abreu, João Capistrão de. *Os caminhos antigos e povoamento do Brasil*. Rio de Janeiro: Edição da Sociedade Capistrão de Abreu, Livraria Briguiet, 1930.

    The portion dealing with Solís and the earliest routes into the interior is pertinent. By one of Brazil's most eminent historians.

240. ———. *O descobrimento do Brasil*. Rio de Janeiro: Ediçao da Sociedade Capistrano de Abreu, Annuario do Brasil, 1929.

    Based on contemporary and good standard secondary sources.

241. ———. *O Descobrimento do Brasil e seu desenvolvimento no seculo XVI* (These do concurso). Rio de Janeiro: G. Leuzinger e filhos, 1883.

A short work, dealing with some of the historical problems concerning the discovery of Brazil.

242. ———. *O descobrimento do Brasil pelos portuguezes.* Rio de Janeiro: Laemmert a Cia., 1900.

An enlarged version of an article published in the *Jornal do Commercio*, May 3, 1900.

243. Alemida, Washington Perry de. "Cristovão Jacques e sua expedicão ao Brasil." *Revista do Instituto Histórico e Geográfico Brasileiro*, 287 (abr.-jun., 1970): 439-48.

An account of Jacques' coastal patrol operations along the Brazilian coast of interest in connection with survivors of the Solís expedition.

244. Brandenburger, Clemente. "O Descobrimento do Brasil por Vincente Yáñez Pinzón." *Revista do Instituto Histórico e Geográfico Brasileiro*, 175 (1941): 155-67.

245. Cortesão, Jaime. *Cabral e as origens do Brasil.* Rio de Janeiro: Edição do Ministerio das Relações Exteriores, 1944.

By a strong defender of Portuguese priority of discovery. Deals with historic topography.

246. ———. *A expedicão de Pedro Alvares Cabral e o descobrimento do Brasil.* Lisboa: Aillaud e Bertrand, 1922.

A good, critical study of Cabral's discovery of Brazil.

247. Coutinho, Carlos Veigas Gago. "O 'acuso' de Cabral. Reflexões tecnicas." *Boletim da Sociedade Geográfica de Lisboa*, 74 (oct.-dez. 1956): 355-410.

By a Portuguese admiral and scholar. Claims that Cabral's discovery was not accidental, since the Portuguese had discovered Brazil in 1497, and possibly earlier.

248. Destefani, Laurio H. "Expediciones espanolãs en las costas del Brazíl en las primeras décadas del siglo

XVI: núcleos de poblaciones y acaecimientos principales." *Revista do Instituto Histórico e Geográfico Brasileiro*, 287 (abr.-jun. 1970): 251-96.

Includes a bibliography. Deals with early Spanish exploration and reconnaissance along the coast.

249. Ferreira, Vieira. "O Cosmógrafo Martin Behaim e o descobrimento do Brasil." *Revista do Instituto Histórico e Geográfico Brasileiro*, 219 (abr.-jun. 1953): 79-105.

    Presents the extraordinary claim that Martin Behaim had explored the coast of Brazil, proceeded south, and discovered the Strait of Magellan in 1484-85.

250. Fleiuss, Max. "O Brasil e seu descobrimento." *Revista do Instituto Histórico e Geográfico Brasileiro*, 186 (jan.-mar. 1945): 39-54.

251. Gaffarel, Paul. *Les français au delà des mers. Les découvreurs français du XIVe au XVIe siècle. Côtes de Guinée, du Brésil, et de l'Amérique du Nord.* Paris, 1889.

    By an authority on the French in Brazil; assigns France priority in the discovery of America.

252. Greenlee, William B. *The Voyage of Pedro Alvares Cabral to Brazil and India, from Contemporary Documents and Narratives.* Trans. with Introduction and notes by W.B. Greenlee. London: Bernard Quaritch for the Hakluyt Society, 1938.

    Greenlee believes that Cabral, sailing farther west to shorten the time for his voyage, reached the coast of Brazil by accident and was the first European to do so.

253. Guedes, Max Justo. "As primeiras expedições portuguêsas e o reconhecimento da coast brasileira." *Revista do Instituto Histórico e Geográfico Brasileiro*, 287 (1ª parte, 1970): 133-200.

    A detailed study of the 1500-04 voyages, with discussion of cartography and a bibliography.

254. ———. "O reconhecimento do litoral brasileiro na 1ª década do século XVI: duas cartas pouco estudadas: Francisco Rodrigues--c. 1513 e Piri Réis--1513. *Revista do Instututo Histórico e Geográfico Brasileiro*, 287 (abr.-jun. 1970): 463-67.

255. Hernández-Pinzón y Ganzimotto, José L. *Vicente Yáñez Pinzón: sus viajes y descubrimientos*. Madrid: Imprenta del Ministerio de Marina, 1920.

    A brief account, largely based on Navarette, by a Spanish marine captain.

256. Leite, Duarte. *Descubridores do Brasil*. Porto: Livraria Lello, Ltda., 1931.

    Describes the supposed voyage of Duarte Pacheco to Brazil, yet refuses to acknowledge the presence of Vicente Yáñex Pinzón, Alonso de Ojeda, Diego de Lepe, or Amerigo Vespucci.

257. Martins Filho, Enéas. "A expedição de 1500." *Revista do Instituto Histórico e Geográfico Brasileiro*, 289 (abr.-jun. 1970) 20-35.

    The Cabral expedition.

258. Nowell, Charles E. "The Discovery of Brazil--Accidental or Intentional?" *Hispanic American Historical Review*, 16 (Aug. 1936): 311-38.

    Presents arguments for the discovery of Brazil by the Portuguese before 1492; suggests that Cabral was to explore the coast and establish Portuguese sovereignty.

259. Pombo, José Francisco da Rocha. *História do Brasil*. 10 vols. Rio de Janeiro: Fonseca Saraiva, 1905. (9ª ed., revised by Hélio Vianna, Rio de Janeiro: Edições Melhoramentos, 1960.)

    One of the most extensive general histories of Brazil. Vol. 1, Part 1, Ch. 3 deals with Cabral; Vol. 1, Part 2 Chs. 1, 2 cover the early discoveries.

260. Solnick, Bruce B. "The Discovery and Early Settlement of Brazil and the Spanish Caribbean: a Study in Contrasts." *Revista do Instituto Histórico e Geográfico Brasileiro*, 287 (oct.-dez. 1970): 479-82.

261. Souza, Thomaz Oscar Marcondes de. "A concepção geográfica dos portuguêses após o descobrimento de América." *Revista de História*, 26 (São Paulo, jan.-mar. 1963): 145-63.

   Discounts any Portuguese idea of a continent from the discovery of Brazil, since Pero Vaz de Caminha described it as an island.

262. ―――. *O descubrimento do Brasil. Estudo crítico de acordo com a documentação histórico-cartográfica e a náutica.* (Brasiliana, 253) São Paulo: Companhia Editora Nacional, 1946. 2^a ed., 1956.

   Supports the accidental discovery by Cabral thesis; does not accept any prior discovery.

263. ―――. "A divulgação pela imprensa da noticia do descobrimento do Brasil por Alvares Cabral." *Revista de História*, 28 (58) (São Paulo, abr.-jun. 1964): 389-404.

264. ―――. "Um suposto descobrimento do Brasil antes de 1498." *Revista de História*, 25 (Sao Paulo, jul.-set. 1962): 439-68.

   Asserts that the "authentic island" (supposedly Brazil, but the longitude is wrong) appearing on the Andrea Bianco portolan of 1498 was one of the Cape Verde Islands.

265. Vigneras, Louis-André. "El viaje al Brasil de Alonso Vélez de Mendoza y Luis Guerra (1500-1501)." *Anuario de Estudios Americanos*, 14 (1957): 333-50.

   Vigneras believes that this was the first voyage south of C. São Agostinho unless Vespucci was there in 1499.

266. Vogt, John L., Jr. "Portuguese Exploration in Brazil and the Feitora System, 1500-1530: the First Economic

Cycle of Brazilian History." Ph.D. Diss., University of Virginia, 1957. 28/07-A, p. 2635, BFJ67-17630.

2. The Amazon region.

  a. Primary sources.

267. Carvajal, Fr. Gaspar de. *Descubrimiento del río de las Amazonas según la relación de Fr. Gaspar de Carvajal, con otros documentos.* Con introducción por José Toribio Medina. Sevilla: Imprenta de E. Rasco, 1894. English translation by Bertram T. Lee as *The Discovery of the River Amazon According to the Account of Friar Gaspar Carvajal.* New York: American Geographical Society, 1934.

An invaluable source, written by a participant. The lengthy introduction by Chile's most productive historian is excellent.

  b. Secondary sources.

268. Albornoz, Miguel. *Orellana, el caballero de las Amazonas.* Quito: Biblioteca Ecuatoriana de "Ultimas Noticias," 1946.

The work of a competent scholar, based on the sources, but undocumented.

269. Andrade, Francisco. "Descubridores y conquistadores del Amazonas." *Boletín de Historia y Antiguedades,* 29 (Bogotá, feb.-mar. 1942): 200-37. Academia Colombiana de Historia, *Conferencias* (1941-42): 131-68.

An outline of Spanish and Portuguese voyages of discovery and exploration to 1692.

270. Gil Munilla, Ladislao. *Descubrimiento del Marañón.* Prólogo de D. Amando Melón. Sevilla: Escúela de Estudies Hispano-Americanos de Sevilla, 1954.

Contains useful maps and charts; provides a solution to the problem of the location of the Marañón. Chiefly concerned with land exploration.

271. ———. "Diego de Lepe, descubridor del Marañón." *Anuario de Estudios Americanos*, 9 (Sevilla, 1952): 73-99.

States that Pinzón discovered the Amazon, but that Lepe discovered the Marañón, which is the Pará River (not to be confused with the upper Amazon in Peru).

272. "El IV centenario del descubrimiento del río de las Amazonas." *Boletín de las Sociedad Geográfica de Lima*, Número extraordinario correspondiente al tomo LIX, 1942.

A collection of articles celebrating the four hundredth anniversary of the discovery of the Amazon.

273. Markham, Sir Clements R., ed. *Expeditions into the Valley of the Amazons*, 1539-40. London: The Hakluyt Society, 1859.

The original 1639 edition, reprinted and edited by a well-respected authority on South America.

274. Means, Philip A. "Gonzalo Pizarro and Francisco de Orellana." *Hispanic American Historical Review*, 14 (1934): 275-95.

3. The northern coasts.

a. Primary sources.

275. Andagoya, Pascual de. *Narrative of the Proceedings of Pedrarias Dávila in the Provinces of Tierra Firme or Castilla del Oro, and of the Discovery of the South Sea and the Coasts of Peru and Nicaragua*. Trans. and ed. by Clements R. Markham. London: The Hakluyt Society, 1865.

A brief volume, very useful, with an excellent introduction.

276. Enciso, Martín Fernández de. *Suma de Geografía*. (Sevilla, 1519.) Reprinted as *Descripción de las Indias Occidentales*, with an introduction by José Toribio Medina. Santiago de Chile, 1897. Also appears as *A Brief Summe of Geographie*. Ed. with introduction and notes by E.G.R. Taylor. London: The Hakluyt Society, 1932.

An excellent description by a lawyer of Hispaniola, who was a partner of Alonso de Ojeda and Diego Necuesa.

b. Secondary sources.

277. Abrahams, Enrique G. "Vasco Núñez de Balboa y el nuevo océano." *Lotería*, 11 (130) (Panamá, set. 1966): 80-93.

278. Altoaguirre y Duvale, Angel de. *Vasco Náñez de Balboa. Estudio Histórico*. Madrid: Real Academia de Historia, 1914.

   Most of this valuable study is an appendix of 80 original documents and MSS. from 1508-1525.

279. Anderson, Charles L.G. *Life and Letters of Vasco Nunez de Balboa*. New York: Fleming H. Revell Co., 1941.

   A good, useful biography.

280. Anderson, Gerald. "Alonso de Ojeda: su primer viaje de exploración." *Revista de Indias*, 20 (79) (Madrid, enero-marzo 1960): 13-64.

   An excellent study. Claims that the expedition landed at C. Orange in Amapá, then sailed westward along the coast to Colombia. Ojeda was in command; Vespucci merely accompanied him.

281. Andresco, Víctor. *Juan de la Cosa, autor del primer mapa de América*. Madrid: Editorial "Gran Capitán," 1949.

   One of the few biographies of this great cartographer.

282. Ballesteros y Beretta, Antonio. *La marina cantabra y Juan de la Cosa*. Santander: Diputación Provincial, 1954.

   A good study. Pp. 183-404 are pertinent.

283. Bayle, Constantino, S.J. *Alonso de Hojeda*. Madrid: Administración de "Razón y Fé," 1925.

A good, brief, popular account by a competent historian.

284. Camin, Alfonso. *Juan de la Cosa*. México: Revista Norte, 1945.

   A good, useful biography.

285. García, Casiano. *Vida del Comendador Diego de Ordaz, descubridor del Orinoco*. Mexico, Editora Justicia, 1952.

   Covers Ordaz' service under Cortes and in the Orinoco region.

286. Harlow, Vincent T., ed. *The Discoverie of Guiana by Sir Walter Raleigh*. London: Argonaut Press, 1928.

   An edited version of Raleigh's account, which also appears in Richard Hakluyt, *Principall Navigations*.... Vol. 10 (Item 40). The introduction has an excellent essay on the quest for El Dorado.

287. Irving, Washington. *Voyages and Discoveries of the Companions of Columbus*. New York: Ungar, 1960.

   An interesting, well-written account, based on the sources available. Includes the exploits of Alonso de Ojeda, Peralonso Niño, Cristóbal Guerra, Vincente Yáñez Pinzón, Diego de Lepe, Rodrigo de Bastidas, Diego Nicuesa, Vasco Núñez de Balboa, Pedro de Valdivia, and Juan Ponce de León.

288. Medina, José Toribio. *El descubrimiento del Océano Pacífico. Vasco Núñez de Balboa, Hernando de Magallanes y sus compañeros*. 2 vols. in 1. Santiago de Chile: Imprenta Universitaria, 1913-14.

   By Chile's most distinguished historian. The first volume is devoted entirely to Balboa.

289. Navarrete, Martín Fernández de. *Viajes de los españoles por la costa de Paria*. Con dos mapas. Madrid: Calpe, 1923.

   By the great Spanish historian of discovery. Complements Item 287.

290. Nectario Maria, hermano. "Descubrimiento y primera expedición al Valle del Río Boconó; año 1548." *Boletín de la Academia Nacional de Historia* 46 (182) (abr.-jun. 1963): 287-292.

291. Nowell, Charles E. "The Discovery of the Pacific: a Suggested Change of Approach." *Pacific Historical Review*, 16 (Feb. 1947): 1-10.

 Assigns priority of discovery over Vasco Núñez de Balboa to the Portuguese António de Abreu, who sailed from Malacca in 1511, November, and entered the Pacific Ocean soon after.

292. Ramos, Demetrio. "Alonso de Ojeda, en el gran proyecto de 1501 y en tránsito del sistema de descubrimiento y rescate al de poblamiento." *Boletín de la Academia Nacional de Historia,* 50 (197) (Caracas, enero-marzo 1967): 34-85.

 A good study, with a valuable bibliography.

293. Romoli, Kathleen. *Balboa of Darién: Discoverer of the Pacific.* New York: Doubleday & Co., 1953.

 A lively biography, with useful maps, but not always historical.

294. ———. "De Darién a la Mar del Sur. Fuentes, Interpretaciones, y Hechos del Viaje de Vasco Núñez de Balboa." *Boletín de Historia y Antigüedades,* 47 (Bogotá, 1960): 16-35.

 A valuable study, with maps showing Balboa's route of discovery.

295. Seco, Carlos. "Algunos datos definitivos sobre el viaje Hojeda-Vespúcio. *Revista de Indias,* 15 (Madrid, enero-marzo 1955): 89-107.

 Holds that Amerigo Vespucci did not command an expedition in 1499; he sailed with Alonso de Ojeda, and left him to explore on his own.

* Solnick, Bruce B. "The Discovery and Early Settlement of Brazil and the Spanish Caribbean: a Study in Contrasts." *Revista do Instituto Histórico e*

Geográfico Brasileiro, 287 (oct.-nov. 1970): 479-82.

Item 260.

296. Tobon Betancur, Julio. "La historia de Antioguia comienza en Urubá." *Lotería*, 11 (131) (Panamá, oct. 1966): 73-82.

297. Vigneras, Louis-André. *The Discovery of South America and the Andalusian Voyages*. Chicago: University of Chicago Press, 1976.

   A very important study, based on the Spanish Notarial Archives. Details the voyages of those whom Washington Irving called "the companions of Columbus," nearly all of which originated in Sevilla, and shows how these voyages were business enterprises as well as voyages of discovery. Vigneras accepts two of Amerigo Vespucci's voyages.

298. ———. "The Three Brothers Guerra of Triana and their Five Voyages to the New World." *Hispanic American Historical Review*, 52 (Nov. 1927): 621-41.

   Gives a chronology of the Andalusian voyages and a detailed account of the Guerra vayages.

4. Southeastern South America.

   a. Primary sources.

299. "Asiento de la gente y pasajeros que fueron en la armada que llevá al Rió de la Plata su gobernador Don Pedro de Mendoza. 1535. (Copy from the Archivo General de Indias, Sevilla.) *Revista de la Biblioteca Nacional*, 6 (21-22) (Buenos Aires, 1942): 177-203.

   b. Secondary sources.

300. Barclay, William Singer. *The Land of Magellan*. New York: Brentano's, 1926.

   A useful account, containing two maps of the Strait.

301. Biddle, Richard. *A Memoir of Sebastian Cabot....* London: Hurst, Chance & Co., 1831.

A thorough account of Cabot's voyages, based on the original sources.

302. Gallez, Pablo J. "Cristóbal de Haro y el descubrimiento del Estrecho Magallanes en 1514." Academia Nacional de Historia, Buenos Aires, *Investigaciones y Ensayos*, 17 (1974): 313-30.

    Maintains that Haro, sailing with the fleet of João of Lisboa in 1513 "around Brazil," actually passed through the Strait. Schöner's globe, made shortly afterward, is submitted as evidence; it shows the Strait in V form, before the voyage of Magellan.

303. Gandía, Enrique de. "Descubrimiento del Río de la Plata, del Paraguay, y del Estrecho de Magallanes." Junta de HIstoria y Numismática Americana, *Historia de la Nación Argentina*. Buenos Aires: Imprenta de la Universidad, 1932. Vol. 2, Ch. 3, 553-610.

    A brief, scholarly account.

304. ———. "Las Islas Argentinas de San Antonio." *Revista Geográfica Argentina*, 24 (no. 1945): 265-70.

    Explains his thesis that Duarte Barbosa discovered the Malvinas or Falkland Islands.

305. Groussac, Paul. "La edpedición de Mendoza." República Argentina, *Anales de la Biblioteca*, 7 (1912): ix-clxxviii.

    An excellent account, with 300 pages of documents from the Archivo General de Indias in Sevilla.

306. Harisse, Henry. *John Cabot, the Discoverer of North America, and Sebastian His Son*. London: B.F. Stevens, 1896.

    An excellent study by an outstanding authority. Part 2, Chs. 1, 6, and 10 are pertinent.

307. Laguardia Trías, Rolando A. *El predescubrimiento del Río de la Plata por la Expedición Portuguesa de 1511-12*. Lisboa: Junta de Investigações do Ultramar, 1973.

This is the Esteban Froes expedition, which Col. Laguardia Trías believes may have been identical with the Cristóbal Haro expedition. The book is extremely well-documented, and presents many documents hitherto unpublished.

308. Markham, Sir Clements R. *Early Spanish Voyages to the Strait of Magellan.* London: The Hakluyt Society, 1911.

Includes the voyages of García Jofré do Loaysa, Sebastian de Elcano, Alvarez de Sayavedra, Simón de Alcanzaba, the Bishop of Plasencia expedition, and Bartolomé García de Nodal and Gonzalo de Nodal.

309. Medina, José Toribio. *Algunas noticias de León Pancaldo, y su tentativa para ir desde Cádiz al Perú por el estrecho de Magallanes en los años de 1537-1538.* Santiago de Chile: Imprenta de Elzeviriana, 1908.

A brief (33 pp.) but very well-documented account of the unsuccessful attempt of a Genoese mariner to sail through the Strait.

310. ———. *Juan Díaz de Solís, estudio histórico.* 2 vols. Santiago de Chile, 1897.

A first-rate work by Chile's leading historian. Vol. 1 consists of a historical introduction, vol. 2 is a collection of documents.

311. ———. *El veneciano Sebastián Caboto.* 2 vols. Santiago de Chile: Imprenta Universitaria, 1908.

Perhaps the best biography of Cabot, thoroughly documented, also including biographies of those who sailed with him. Excellent on the Rio de la Plata expedition.

312. ———. *Los viajes de Diego García de Moguer al Río de la Plata.* Santiago de Chile: Imprenta Elziviriana, 1908.

An excellent work containing numerous documents. García de Moguer sailed with Juan de Solís, Ferdinand Magellan, and Sebastian Cabot.

313. Monteiro, Mario. *Aleixo Garcia. Descobridor portuguez do Paraguay e da Bolivia, em 1524-25.* Lisboa: H.E.G. de Carvalho, 1923.

    A brief account of this important explorer.

314. Naia, Alexandre Gaspar de. "Quem foi o primeiro descobridor do Rio da Prata e da Argentina?" *Revista de História,* 20 (41) (São Paulo, jan.-mar. 1968): 65-83.

315. Nowell, Charles E. "Aleixo Garcia and the White King." *Hispanic American Historical Review,* 26 (Nov. 1926): 450-66.

    An excellent essay on the first European to reach the Inca realm.

316. Pastells, Pablo. S.J. *El descubrimiento del Estrecho de Magallanes.* 2 vols. Madrid: Sucesores de Rivadeneyra Artes Gráficas, 1920.

    An excellent piece of scholarship, by a former director of the Archivo de Indias in Sevilla. It considers not only the discovery of the Strait, but also early voyages of exploration in the area. There is an appendix of documents.

   5. The Pacific coast.

      a. Primary sources.

317. Ladrillero, Juan Fernández de. "Relación." *Anuario Hidrográfico de la Marina,* Año VI. Santiago de Chile, 1880.

318. López de Gómara, Francisco. "El descubrimiento de Chile." *Boletín de la Academia Chilena de Historia,* 7 (1936): 143-46.

    A reprint of the account by a sixteenth-century historian.

319. Valdivia, Pedro de. "Cartas de Pedro de Valdivia que tratan del descubrimiento y conquista de Chile." *Biblioteca de Autores Españoles,* Vol. 131. Madrid: Ediciones Atlas, 1960.

320. Zárate, Agustín de. "Almagro y el descubrimiento de Chile." *Boletín de la Academia Chilena de Historia*, 7 (1936): 132-42.

    The account by the distinguished sixteenth-century historian.

    b. Secondary sources.

321. Greve, Ernesto. "Estudio histórico-geográfico sobre las viajes de Gómez de alvarado, Pedro de Valdivia, Francisco de Villagra y García Hurtado de Mendoza hacia el sur." *Revista Chilena de Historia y Geográfia*, 74 (set.-dic. 1933): 571-637.

    Includes the voyage of Juan Bautista Pastene as well; disputes his claim that he reached Chiloé I.

322. Markham, Clements R. *Reports on the Discovery of Peru*. London: The Hakluyt Society, 1872.

    An edited volume, with introduction and notes on the early accounts of discovery.

323. Medina, José Toribio. *Bartolomé Ruíz de Andrade, primer piloto del mar del sur*. Santiago de Chile: Imprenta Elziviriana, 1919.

    A scholarly study of Francisco Pizarro's pilot.

324. ———. *El piloto Juan Fernández*. Santiago de Chile: Imprenta Elziviriana, 1918.

    An excellent work on this important navigator, who was possibly the discoverer of Chile.

325. Murphy, Robert C. "The Earliest Spanish Advances Southward from Panamá along the West Coast of South America." *Hispanic American Historical Review*, 21 (Feb. 1941): 3-28.

    An account of the pre-conquest expeditions along the Pacific coast from Panamá to Tumbes.

326. Ramón Folch, José Armando de. *Descubrimiento de Chile, y compañeros de Almagro*. Santiago de Chile:

Instituto de Investigaciones Historicos, 1953 (i.e., 1954)

Provides biographical data based on sources available in Chile for 178 of the 500 or so who were with Almagro.

327. ―――. "Las naves de Almagro en el descubrimiento de Chile." *Boletín de la Academia Chilena de la Historia*, 65 (1961): 170-78.

D. The conquest and the late sixteenth century.

1. General.

a. Primary sources.

328. Léry, Jean. *Historia Navigationis in Brasiliam, qvae et America dicitvr. Qva describitvr avtoris navigatio, qvaiqve in mare vidit memoriae prodenda: Villagagnonis in America gesta....* Geneva: Evstathivs Vignon, 1586. A French edition as *Histoire d'un voyage fait en la Terre du Brésil, autrement dite Amérique*, edited by J.C. Morisot, was reprinted in Genève in 1975.

An account of the attempt of the French to found a colony in Brazil called "Antarctic France." The Latin edition contains 7 woodcuts and a folded plate depicting a battle scene. Léry was a naturalist and a Calvinist.

329. Nieuhoff, John. *Voyages and Travels into Brazil and the East-Indies, containing an Exact Description of Dutch Brazil, and Divers Parts of the East Indies.* (Vol. 2 of Churchill, Anshawn, *A Collection of Voyages & Travels*...London: Lintot & Osborn, 1744. Cited above as Item 36.)

Based on nine years' residence in Brazil and the East Indies.

330. Staden, Hans. *The True History of His Captivity, 1557.* Trans. and ed. by Malcolm Letts. London: George Routledge & Sons, Ltd., 1928.

An excellent, colorful account of his captivity by Brazilian Indians. He was a Hessian gunner in the Portuguese service.

b. Secondary sources.

331. Descola, Jean. *The Conquistadors*. Trans. by Malcolm Barnes. London: Allen & Unwin, 1954.

    A good, popular account.

332. Kirkpatrick, Frederick A. *The Spanish Conquistadores*. London, A.C. Black, 1934.

    The best general account available. The Appendix contains a useful list of monies and weights.

333. Pizarro y Orellana, Fernando. *Varones ilustres del Nvevo mvndo....* Madrid: D. Díaz de la Carrera, 1639.

    Includes Colombus, Alonso de Ojeda, Diego de Almagro, Diego García de Paredes, and the Pizarros. A legal and political discourse, intending primarily to glorify the Pizarros.

334. Richman, Irving B. *The Spanish Conquerors: a Chronicle of the Dawn of Empire Overseas*. New Haven: Yale University Press, 1919.

    A good, scholarly introduction.

2. The Amazon region.

a. Primary sources.

335. Alvarez Maldonado, Juan. *Relación de la jornada y descubrimiento del río Manu (hoy Madre de Dios) por Juan Alvarez Maldonado en 1567.* Sevilla: Imprenta de C. Salas, 1899.

336. Barbot, Jean. *A Description of the Coasts of North and South Guinea, and of Ethiopia Inferior, . . . and a New Relation of the Province of Guiana, and of the Great Rivers of Amazons & Oronoque in South America.* (Vol. 5 of Churchill, Awnshawn, *A Collection of Voyages and Travels....* London: Lintot & Osborn, 1732. Cited above as Item 36.

337. Bollaert, William, ed. *The Expedition of Pedro de Ursua and Lope de Aguirre.* London: The Hakluyt Society, 1861.

    An excellent edition of this colorful tale.

338. Simón, Pedro, O.F.M. *Historial de la expedición de Pedro de Ursua al Marañón y de las aventuras de Lope de Aguirre.* Lima: Sanmartí y Cía., 1942.

    b. Secondary sources.

339. Breymann, Walter N. "The Opening of the Amazon, 1540-1640." Ph.D. Diss., 10/40, p. 188. BFJ00-02059. University of Illinois, 1950.

340. Burmester, Luis Germán. *Lope de Aguirre y la jornada de los Marañones.* Buenos Aires: Librería "Menéndez," 1941.

341. Jos, Emiliano. *La expedición de Ursúa al Dorado, la rebelión de Lope de Aguirre, y el itinerario de los "Marañones."* Huesca: V. Campo, 1927.

    Thesis extract. Based on unedited MSS. and documents.

  3. Northern South America.

    a. Primary sources.

342. Federmann, Nikolaus. *Narración del primer viaje de Federmann a Venezuela.* Caracas: Tipografía del Comercio, 1916.

    An invaluable source.

343. Harcourt, Robert. A *Relation of a Voyage to Guiana.* London: The Hakluyt Society, 1928.

    Harcourt's colonizing voyage, 1608-09. An Appendix presents a report on the Marwin (Maroni) R. made to Harcourt.

344. Keymis, Laurence. A *Relation of the Second Voyage to Guiana, Performed and Written in the Yeare 1596.* Appears in Hakluyt, Richard, *Principal*

Fifteenth- and Sixteenth-Century Exploration 63

Navigations.... (Item 40), Vol. 10.

The account of the expedition sent out by Sir Walter Raleigh to investigate the Río Caroní as a possible route to El Dorado.

345. Raleigh, Sir Walter. *The Discoverie of the Large, Rich and Beautifull Empire of Guiana, with a Relation of the Great and Golden Citie of Manoa (Which the Spaniards call El Dorado) and the Provinces of Emeria, Aromaia, Amapaia, and other Countries, with Their Rivers Adjoining*.... Appears in Hakluyt, Richard, *Principall Navigations*.... (Item 40), Vol. 10.

Raleigh's exaggerated account of Guiana; the source of the fable concerning the mythical Lake Parima and the "golden city" of Manoa.

346. Simón, Pedro, O.F.M. *Noticias historiales de las conquistas de Tierra Firme en las Indias occidentales*, 3 vols. Bogotá: Medardo Rivas, 1882-92.

A very valuable source, based in part of Juan de Castellanos' *Historia de la Nueva Granada*, now lost. Fray Simón was not a participant in the conquests, but knew many of those who were, and knew the country well.

b. Secondary sources.

347. Arciniegas, Germán. *Germans in the Conquest of America: a Sixteenth Century Venture*. Trans. by Angel Flores. New York: Macmillan Co., 1943.

A useful account, but marked by an anti-German bias.

348. Ariza, Alberto E. "Itinerario cronológico y geográfico de la expedición de Jiménez de Quesada al Reino de Chibcha." *Boletín Cultural y Bibliográfico*, 6 (7) (Bogotá, 1963): 984-97.

Contains a useful bibliography.

349. Born, Franz. *Auf der Suche nach dem goldenen Gott. Orellana entdeckt den Amazonas*. Berlin: Verlag der Natim, 1952.

A brief, popular account of the search for "el Dorado."

350. Fernández Piedrahita, Lucas. *Historia general de las conquistas del Nuevo Reyno de Granada*. Amberes, Juan Baptista Verdussen, 1688.

   Bishop Fernández Piedrahita of Panamá compiled much of this from MSS. of Gonzalo Jiménez de Quesada, no longer extant. There is no direct documentation. Only the first part, to 1564, was published.

351. Friede, Juan. *Descubrimiento del Nuevo Reino de Granada y Fundación de Bogotá (1536-39)*. Bogotá: Banco de la Republica, 1960.

   A basic work by one of Colombia's leading historians. Contains new information from the Archivo de Indias.

352. ———. "Geographical Ideas and the Conquest of Venezuela." *The Americas*, 16 (Oct. 1959): 145-59.

   Covers early geographical concepts of America, the legend of El Dorado, and geographical ideas of the Andes.

353. ———. *Gonzalo Jiménez de Quesada a través de documentos históricos*. Bogotá: Editorial ABC. 1960.

   A very well-documented biography of the *conquestador*, by one of Colombia's leading historians. A basic work.

354. ———. "Jiménez de Quesada e el descubrimiento." *Revista de América* 23 (Bogotá, dic. 1951): 660-74.

355. ———. *Vida y viajes de Nicolás Federmann, conquistador, poblador, y cofundador de Bogotá, 1506-1542*. Bogotá: Ediciones Libreria Buchholz, 1960.

   An excellent, well-documented life of this German *conquistador*.

356. Graterón, Daniel. "Hombres de la conquista--Nicolás de Federmann." *Boletín del Centro Histórico Larense*, Año III, No. 10 (abr.-jun. 1944): 82-89.

357. Haebler, Konrad. *Die Überseeischen Unternehmungen der Welser*. Leipzig, C.L. Hirschfeld, 1903.

    An account of the Welsers' enterprise in Venezuela.

358. Humbert, Jules. *L'Occupation Allemande du Venezuela au XVI Siècle, Période dite des Welser, 1528-56*. Bordeaux, 1905.

    A French view of the Welser enterprise; contains a valuable map.

359. Oviedo y Baños, José de. *Historia de la conquista y población de la provincia de Venezuela*. (Vol. 107, *Biblioteca de Autores Españoles*.) Madrid: Ediciones Atlas, 1926.

    Written in 1723. The author was a great story teller, who delighted in poetic episodes and the lives of saintly people.

360. Pérez Embid, Florentino. *Diego de Ordas, compañero de Cortes, y explorador del Orinoco*. Sevilla: Escuela de Estudios Hispano-Americano, 1950.

    A brief but very useful biography. Half of the volume consists of documents.

361. Restrepo Tirado, Ernesto. *Descubrimiento y conquista de Colombia*. 2 vols. Bogotá: Imprenta Nacional, 1917-19.

    A good, well-written, extensive account.

362. Schuller, Rudolf. *The Ordaz and Dortal Expeditions in Search of El-Dorado, as Described on Sixteenth Century Maps*. Smithsonian Miscellaneous Collections, Vol. 66, No. 4. Washington, D.C., The Smithsonian Institution, 1916.

    A 15-page publication of excellent maps.

363. Vila, Marco Aurelio. "El primer viaje de Nicolás Federmann vista por la geografía." *Revista Nacional de Cultura*, 22 (Caracas, mayo-agosto 1960): 140-41.

4. Southern South America.

a. Primary sources.

364. Domínguez, Luis L., ed. *The Conquest of the River Plate* (1535-1555). London: The Hakluyt Society, 1891.

Includes the voyage of Ulrich Schmidt and the Commentaries of Alvar Núñez Cabeza de Vaca.

365. Hawkins, Richard. *The Observations of Sir Richard Hawkins, k^{nt}.. in His Voyage into the South Sea in the Year 1593*. London: The Hakluyt Society, 1847.

366. Núñez Cabeza de Vaca, Alvar. *Commentaires d'Alvar Núñez Cabeça de Vaca, adelante et gouverneur du Rio de la Plata, rédigé par Pero Hernandez, notaire et secrétaire de la province*. Valladolid, 1555; Paris: A Bertrand, 1837. *Comentarios de Alvar Núñez Cabeza de Vaca*. Vol. 22, *Biblioteca de Autores Españoles*. Madrid: Ediciones Atlas, 1946.

Two good editions of this great classic. An earlier Spanish edition may be found in Barcia Carballido y Zuñiga, Andres, *Historiadores primitivos de las Indias occidentales* (Item 34).

367. Sarmiento de Gamboa, Pedro. *Viage al Estrecho de Magallanes ... en los Años de 1579 y 1580*. Madrid: Imprenta Real de la Gazeta, 1768. (An English translation by Sir Clements Markham appears as *Narratives of the Voyages of Pedro Sarmiento de Gamboa to the Straits of Magellan*. London: The Hakluyt Society, 1895.)

368. Schmidel (Schmidt), Ulrich. *Vera historia....* Noribergae: Hulsin, 1599. Subsequent translations: *Histoire véritable d'un voyage curieux, fait par Ulrich Schmidel de Straubing, dans l'Amérique ou le Nouveau monde, par le Brésil, et le Rio de la Plata*

depuis l'année 1534 jusqu'en 1554. Paris: A. Bertrand, 1873; *Viaje Al Río de la Plata*. Notas por Bartolomé Mitre, tr. por Samuel Lafona Quevada. Buenos Aires: Cabaut y Cia., 1903; *The Conquest of the River Plate, 1535-1555. Voyage of Ulrich Schmidt to the Rivers La Plata and Paraguai*. London: The Hakluyt Society, 1891; *Viaje al Río de la Plata*. 2^a ed. Buenos Aires: Emecé, 1945.

A lively, colorful account of the exploration of the Rio de La Plata and the Paraguay R. by a Hessian gunner who accompanied Pedro de Mendoza's expedition and explored with Juan de Ayolas. A new edition was published in Buenos Aires in 1950 as *Viaje al Estrecho de Magallanes (1579-1584). Recopilación de sus relaciones sobre los viajes al estrecho y de sus cartas y memoriales*. 2 vols. Edición y notas de Angel Rosenblatt. Prólogo de Armando Bracen Menéndez. The voyage is well-described in the prologue.

b. Secondary sources.

369. Arciniega, Rosa. *Pedro Sarmiento de Gamboa, el Ulises de América*. Buenos Aires: Editorial Sudamericana, 1956.

A good biography, with a bibliography and list of documents.

370. Bellogín García, Andres. *Vida y hazañas de Alvar Nuñez Cabeza de Vaca*. Madrid: Eitores Voluntad S.A., 1928.

A good, semi-popular biography.

371. Bishop, Morris. *The Odyssey of Cabexa de Vaca*. New York and London: The Century Co., 1933.

A good, scholarly biography of this great explorer. Part II deals with South America.

372. Díaz de Guzmán, Ruy. *La Argentina*. Intro. y notas de Enrique de Gandía. Buenos Aires: Angel Estrada y Cia., 1943.

A very useful work; reprint of the very rare 1835 edition.

373. Gandía, Enrique de. *Historia de la conquista del Río de la Plata y del Paraguay, 1535-1556.* Buenos Aires: A. Garcia Santos, 1932.

   An excellent, scholarly study by one of Argentina's leading and most productive historians.

374. ——— and Manuela Fernández Reyna. *León Pancaldo y la primera expedición genovesa al Río de la Plata.* Buenos Aires, 1952.

   A prize-winning study of this Genoese expedition of 1538.

375. Graham, Robert B. Cunninghame. *The Conquest of the River Plate.* London: Wm. Heinemann, Ltd., 1924.

   The standard account in English; well-written.

376. Groussac, Paul. "Juan de Garay." *Anales de la Biblioteca* 10 (Buenos Aires, 1915): ix-ccc.

   A discussion and appraisal of Garay's work as an explorer and second founder of Buenos Aires. There is appended a lengthy collection of documents relative to the period from the Archivo de Indias in Sevilla.

377. Lafuente Machain, Ricardo de. *Conquistadores del Río de la Plata.* Buenos Aires: Talleres Gráficos de S. de Amorrota e Hijos, 1937.

   A very useful biographical dictionary.

378. Ledesma Medina, Luis A. "El conocimiento del Tucumán y la expedición descubridora de Diego de Rojas." *Revista de la Junta de Estudios Históricos de Santiago del Estero,* 1 (1943): 158-69.

   The story of the exploration of Tucuman by the ill-fated Rojas expedition, searching for the "enchanted city of the Caesars."

379. ———. "Expedición descubridora de Diego de Rojas; Nicolás Heredia dirige la jornada Malaventura--Perú." *Revista de la Junta de Estudios Históricos de Santiago del Estero,* 2 (1944): 37-42.

   The return journey of the ill-fated Rojas expedition.

380. Levillier, Roberto. *Descubrimiento y población del norte argentino por españoles del Perú, 1543-1553.* Buenos Aires: Espasa-Calpe, 1943.

   A good, useful study of the Diego de Rojas expedition by one of Argentina's leading historians.

381. _____. *Nueva crónica de la conquista del Tucumán.* Buenos Aires: "Editores Nosotros," 1926.

   The first of a planned series of 24 volumes, based on materials from the Archivo General de Indias in Sevilla.

382. Lizondo Borda, Manuel. *Descubrimiento del Tucumán, el pasaje de Almagro, la entrada de Rojas, el itinerario de Matienzo.* Tucumán: Universidad Nacional de Tucumán, Instituto de Historia, Lingüistica, y Folklore, 1943.

   A good, brief study, with a map of the route of the expedition of Diego de Rojas.

383. Rubio, Julián Maria. *Exploración y conquista del Río de la Plata.* Siglos XVI y XVII. (Vol. 8, Ballesteros y Beretta, Antonio, ed., *Historia de America.*) Barcelona: Salvat Editores, 1942.

   A comprehensive, scholarly study.

   5. The west coast.

   a. Primary sources.

384. Cieza de León, Pedro de. *La crónica del Perú.* (Vol. 26, *Biblioteca de Autores Españoles.*) Madrid: Ediciones Atlas, 1946. English translations: *The Seventeen Years Travels of Peter de Cieza, Through the Mighty Kingdom of Peru, and the Large Provinces of Cartagena and Popayan in South America, from the City of Panama, on the Isthmus, to the Frontiers of Chile.* London, 1709. *The Travels of Pedro Cieza de Leon, A.D. 1532-50, Contained in the First Part of His Chronicle of Peru.* Trans. and ed. with notes and intro. by Clements R. Markham. London: The Hakluyt Society, 1864.

One of the best accounts of the conquest of Peru, by a Spanish soldier and explorer.

385. Jérez de Salamanca, Francisco. *Verdadera relación de la conquista del Perú y provincia de Cuzco.* Sevilla, 1536. (Vol. 26, *Biblioteca de Autores Españoles.* Madrid: Ediciones Atlas, 1946.) English translation by Clements R. Markham as *Reports on the Discovery of Peru.* London: The Hakluyt Society, 1872.

A brief, eye-witness, official account by Francisco Pizarro's secretary. It ends with the capture of Atahuallpa at Cajamarca.

386. Pizarro, Pedro. *Relación del descubrimiento y conquista de los Reinos del Perú.* (Vol. 168, *Biblioteca de Autores Españoles.*) Madrid: Ediciones Atlas, 1964. English translation by Philip A. Means as *Relation of the Discovery and Conquest of the Kingdom of Peru.* 2 vols. New York: Cortes Society, 1921.

Written by Francisco Pizarro's cousin, who came to Peru with him in 1530 at the age of fifteen. An excellent eyewitness report, written during his old age. The English translation (a limited edition of 250 copies) has an extensive bibliography.

387. *The World Encompassed by Sir Francis Drake Carefully Collected Out of the Notes of Master Francis Fletcher.* London: Nicholas Bourne, 1628. Ann Arbor, Mich.: University Microfilms, 1966. Edited by n.m. Penzer, London: Argonaut Press, 1926.

The authorship of this important account is not certain, but it was probably the work of John Drake, a young cousin of Sir Francis, who accompanied him.

b. Secondary sources.

388. Esteve Barba, Francisco. *Descubrimiento y conquista de Chile.* (Vol. 11 in Ballestero y Beretta, Antonio, ed. *Historia de América.*) Barcelona: Salvat Editorial, 1946.

An excellent study, based on carefully selected sources.

389. García Rosell, Ricardo. *Conquista de la Montaña*. Lima: Tipografía "la Prensa," 1905.

    A brief study of the conquest of the eastern slopes of the Andes.

390. Graham, Robert B. Cunninghame. *Pedro de Valdivia, Conqueror of Chile*. New York: Harper, 1927.

    About one half of this study is text, followed by an Appendix of letters from Valdivia to Emperor Carlos V.

391. Hemming, John. *The Conquest of the Incas*. New York: Harcourt, Brace, Jovanovich, 1970; London: Macmillan, 1970.

    This is an extremely accurate and impartial account of the conquest.

392. Pocock, H.R.S. *The Conquest of Chile*. New York: Stein & Day, 1967.

    A carefully documented work by an Oxford Classics Scholar who spent twenty years in Chile.

393. Prescott, William H. *The Conquest of Peru*. New York: Harper & Brothers, 1847. 2 vols. Partly abridged and revised by Victor W. von Hagen. New York: New American Library, 1961.

    An authoritative classic, based on all the documents available to him. The abridgement is a convenient volume; only the second part, dealing with the civil wars of the conquerors, has been condensed.

394. Ramón Folch, José A. "Gestación del descubrimiento de Chile Central y abandono de su conquista en 1536." *Boletín de la Academia Chilena de la Historia*, 61 (1959): 131-49.

    The Almagro expedition.

395. Rivero y Ustáriz, Mariano Eduardo de and Johann Jakob von Tschudi. *Peruvian Antiquities*. Trans. by Francis L. Hawkes. New York: G.P. Putnam, 1853.

396. Thayer Ojeda, Tomás. *Los Conquistadores de Chile.*
 3 vols. Santiago de Chile: Imprenta Cervantes,
 1900-13.

 An excellent biographical dictionary.

397. Vernon, Ida Stevenson Weldon. *Pedro de Valdivia, Conquistador of Chile.* Austin: University of Texas Institute of Latin American Studies, 1946.

 A good biography, based mainly on José Toribio Medina's *Colección de Documentos inéditos para la historia de Chile* (Item 24).

398. Wilson, Derek. *The World Encompassed. Francis Drake and His Great Voyage.* New York: Harper & Row, 1977.

 A very well written analysis of Sir Francis Drake, scholarly and interesting, but tending to overlook some controversial matters. There are good notes and a bibliography.

VI. SEVENTEENTH- AND EIGHTEENTH-CENTURY EXPLORATION.

A. Exploration in general.

398a. Heawood, Edward. *A History of Geographical Discovery in the Seventeenth and Eighteenth Centuries.*

Cited above as Item 66.

399. *Voyages and Discoveries in South-America....* London: S. Buckley, 1698.

An account of the voyages of Cristóbal de Acuña, Acarete du Biscay, and Jean Grillet and François Bechamel.

B. Eastern South America.

1. Brazil in general.

Abreu, João Capistrano de. *Caminhos antigos e povoamento do Brasil.*

Cited Above as Item 239.

400. Boxer, Charles R. *The Golden Age of Brazil, 1695-1750.* Berkeley and Los Angeles: University of California Press, 1962.

A well-written, carefully documented account of this important period in Brazilian history. The best in English.

401. _____. *Salvador de Sá and the Struggle for Brazil and Angola 1602-1686.* London: University of London, the Athlone Press, 1952.

A first-rate monograph, carefully documented, by an outstanding scholar.

402. Brazil. Primeira Congresso de História Nacional.
História das explorações geográficas. (*Revista do Instituto Histórico e Geográfico Brasileiro.* Tomo Especial, Parte II.) Rio de Janeiro: Imprensa Nacional, 1915.

An excellent collection of articles on the geographical expansion of Brazil to the end of the eighteenth century.

403. Morales Padrón, Francisco. "Los Rusos en Brasil, siglo XVIII." Anuario de Estudios Americanos, 27 (1970): 419-82.

2. The Amazon region.

a. Primary sources.

404. Acuña, Cristóbal de, S.J. *Nuevo descubrimiento del gran río del Amazonas por el P. Cristóbal de Acuña, al cual fue por la provincia de Quito, el ano de 1639.* Quito: Instituto Ecuatoriano de Cultura del Amazonas, 1944. An English translation, *A New Discovery of the Great River of the Amazons* (Madrid: Royal Press, 1641), appears in Clements R. Markham, ed., *Expeditions Into the Valley of the Amazons.* London: The Hakluyt Society.

An excellent, detailed, invaluable account of the Pedro de Teixeira expedition from Belém to Quito, by one of its members.

405. Cortesão, Jaime. "O significado da expedicão de Pedro Teixeira a luz de novos documentos." (Instituto Histórico e Geográfico Brasileiro. IV Congresso Nacional, Abril, 1949. *Anãis*, Terceiro Volume, 169-208.) Rio de Janeiro: Dept. de Imprensa Nacional, 1950.

Three of eight new documents are transcribed. Cortesão believed them sufficient to rank Teixeira among the great intentional builders of Brazil.

406. Teixeira, Pedro de. "Relación del Descubrimiento del Río de las Amazonas." *Boletín de Historia y Antigüedades*, 29 (Bogotá, 1942): 287-307.

Teixeira's own account, along with Martín de
Saavedra y Guzmán's letters to García Méndez de Haro,
President of the Consejo de Indias, to the King, and
the *cédula* to the Viceroy, 1595.

407. Vasconcellos, Luiz Aranha de. "Informação de Luiz
Aranha de Vasconcellos sobre o descobrimento do
Río das Amazonas, 30 de Abril de 1626." *Documentos
para a História da Conquista e Colonisação da Costa
de Leste-Oeste do Brasil,* 391-94. (Vol. 24 of the
Anais da Biblioteca Nacional, Rio de Janeiro, 1905.)

A valuable account of his efforts to establish
Portuguese authority firmly in the lower Amazon River.

408. "Viaje del capitán Pedro Teixeira (1638-1639)."
Boletín de Historia y Antigüedades, 29 (Bogotá,
feb. 1942): 287-307.

Letters of Martín Saavedra y Guzmán and Juan de
Ibarra, with an account of the voyage.

b. Secondary sources.

* Breymann, Walter Norman. "The Opening of the Amazon,
1540-1640." Cited above as Item 339.

409. Church, George Earl, comp. *Explorations Made in the
Valley of the River Madeira from 1744 to 1868.*
London: National Bolivian Navigation Co., 1875.

410. Jiménez de la Espada, Marcos. *Viaje del Capitán
Pedro Teixeira a aguas arriba del río de las
Amazonas, 1638-1639.* Madrid, 1889.

A scholarly work, well-documented.

411. Pagan, Blaise-Francois de, Comte de Merveilles.
*Relation historique et géographique de la grande
Rivière des Amazons dans l'Amérique.* Paris:
Cardin Besogne, 1656. English translation by
William Hamilton, *An Historical and Geographical
Description of the Great Country and River of the
Amazons in America.* London: I. Starkey, 1661.

Based largely on Ácuña, this book was written to try to persuade Cardinal Mazarin to seize the Amazon valley; the English translation was dedicated to Charles II to try to persuade him to seize the basin, since neither Spain, Portugal, nor France had made any serious attempt at occupation.

3. The *bandeirantes* and the *monções*.

   a. Primary sources.

412. Escragnolle Taunay, Affonso de, ed. *Relatos monçoeiros*. São Paulo; Livraria Martins Editôra, 1953.

   A very valuable collection of accounts of the "monsoons."

413. _____. *Rio de Janeiro de Atanho. Impressões de viajantes estrangeiros*. São Paulo: Companhia Editora Nacional, 1942.

   A collection of descriptive accounts by foreign explorers and travelers.

   b. Secondary sources.

414. Buarque de Holanda, Sergio. *Monções*. Coleção Estudos Brasileiros, 3 Serie A. Rio de Janeiro, 1945.

   The best monograph on the subject.

415. Cardozo, Manoel S. "The Last Adventure of Fernão Dias Pair (1674-1681)." *Hispanic American Historical Review*, 26 (1946): 467-79.

   A lively, scholarly account of the last effort of this great *bandeirante*.

416. Cortesão, Jaime. *Rapôso Tavares e a formação territorial do Brasil*. 2 vols. Lisboa: Portugália, 1966.

   Presents this greatest of the *bandeirantes* as a prime mover in the territorial expansion of Brazil westward. There are illustrations and useful maps.

417. Ellis, Alfredo, Jr. *O bandeirismo paulista e o recúo do meridiano*. 3a. ed. São Paulo: Companhia Editora Nacional, 1938.

   A collection of articles published in the *Correiro Paulistano*. There are many citations from documents and several maps.

418. Escragnolle Taunay, Affonso de. *História das bandeiras paulistas*. 2 vols. São Paulo: Edições Melhoramentos, 1953.

   A good condensation of his 11-volume work (Item 419).

419. ———. História geral das bandeiras paulistas. 11 vols. São Paulo: Edições Melhoramentos, 1924-50.

   The standard, classical work on this subject; the most comprehensive study available. Indispensable.

420. Franco, Carvalho. *Bandeiras e bandeirantes de São Paulo*. São Paulo: Companhia Editora Nacional, 1940.

   Shows the extensive operations of the *bandeiras;* a good, systematized approach.

421. Morse, Richard M. *The Bandeirantes: the Historical Role of the Brazilian Pathfinders*. New York: Alfred A. Knopf, 1965.

   A collection of essays and excerpts dealing with this important movement; the best available study in English.

422. Ricardo, Cassiano. "O bandeirante Euclides." *Revista da Academia Paulista de Letras,* Sept. 12, 1947: 98-120.

423. ———. *La marcha hacia el ceste. La influencia de la "bandeira" en la formación social y política del Brasil*. México, D.F.: Fondo de Cultura Econômica, 1956.

   4. Northern South America.

   a. Primary sources.

424. Atkins, John. *A Voyage to Guinea, Brasil, and the West Indies*. London: C. Ward and R. Chandler, 1735.

A descriptive account, with useful information on the northern coast of the continent.

425. Gumilla, Joseph, S.J. *El Orinoco ilustrado, historia natural civil y geográfica de las naciones situades en las riberas del Río Orinoco.* 2 vols. Barcelona: Imprenta Gilbert y Tutó, 1791. 1 vol., Bogotá: Editorial ABC, 1955.

A very valuable work by a Jesuit missionary, describing the valley of the Orinoco and its inhabitants. The original edition contains a useful map and plates; the new edition has several facsimiles.

5. Western South America.

a. Primary sources.

426. Courte de la Blanchardière, René. *A Voyage to Peru: Performed by the Conde of St. Malo, in the Years 1745, 1746, 1747, 1748, and 1749. Written by the Chaplain. To Which Is Added an Appendix, Containing the Present State of the Spanish Affairs in America, in Respect to Mines, Trade, and Discoveries.* London: R. Griffiths, 1753. (English translation of *Nouveau voyage fait au Pérou.* Paris: Imprimérie de Delaguette, 1751.)

A rare, firsthand account, containing valuable information on economic affairs.

427. Mutis, José Celestino. *Diario de observaciones de José Celestino Mutis (1760-1790).* Transcripción, prólogo y notas de Guillermo Hernández de Alba. 2 vols. Bogotá: Editorial Minerva Ltda., 1958.

A valuable reprint of Mutis' botanical work, carefully annotated, with a good introduction.

428. Vargas Ugarte, Rubén, S.J. *Relaciones de viajes (Siglo XVI, XVII, XVIII)* (T. 5 in *Biblioteca Historia Peruana*). Lima: Cia. de Impresiones y Publicidad, 1947.

Contains the journey of Juan de Montemayor from México to Lima, 1617; the journal of a Jesuit exiled from Lima to Cádiz, 1767; and the voyage of five Capuchins from Madrid to Lima, 1710-22.

b. Secondary sources.

429. Frontaura Argandoña, Manuel. *Descubridores y exploradores de Bolivia*. La Paz and Cochhbamba: Editorial "Los Amigos del Libro," 1971.

An excellent study. The bulk of it deals with explorations in the 18th century and after.

430. Steele, Arthur R. *Flowers for the King: the Expedition of Ruiz and Pavón and the "Flora of Peru."* Durham: Duke University Press, 1964.

The best book on the subject, carefully and extensively researched, and very well-written. Illustrated.

6. Southern South America.

a. Primary sources.

431. Acarete du Biscay. *An Account of a Voyage up the River de la Plata and thence over Land to Peru, with Observations on the Inhabitants, as well as Indians and Spaniards, the Cities, Commerce, Fertility, and Riches of that Part of America.* London: Samuel Buckley, 1698.

This brief but valuable work forms a part of *Voyages and Discoveries in South America* (Item 48 above), and was reprinted in 1969 by the Institute Publishing Co., North Haven, Connecticut.

432. Bougainville, Louis-Antoine, comte de. *Voyage autour du monde par la frégate du roi „La Boudeuse„ et la flûte „L'Étoile„ en 1766,67, 68, et 69.* Paris: Chez Saillard & Nyon, 1771. (Translated into English by John Reinhold Forster, F.A.S., as *A Voyage Round the World. Performed by Order of His Most Christian Majesty, in the Years 1766,1768, and 1769.* London: J. Nourse etc., 1772.

An account of the voyage around the world which took him to the Malvinas (Falkland) Is. and the

Strait of Magellan. The French edition contains 18 maps (folded plates), the English edition 5 maps.

433. Byron, John. *The Narrative of the Honourable John Byron* ... *Containing an Account of the Great Distresses Suffered by Himself and His Companions on the Coasts of Patagonia from the Year 1740, Till Their Arrival in England, 1746.* Wigan: W. Bancks, 1784.

   The original account of Commodore Byron's voyage of discovery in the southern hemisphere; interesting is his account of the Patagonian "giants."

434. Dobritzhofer, Martin. *An Account of the Abipones, an Equestrian People of Paraguay.* Translated from the Latin. 3 vols. London: J. Murray, 1822.

   An indispensable source for any study of Paraguay in the eighteenth century.

435. Falkner, Thomas, S.J. *Descripción de Patagonia y de las partes adyacentes de la América Meridional.* Buenos Aires: Imprenta del Estado, 1835.

   This brief volume by an English Jesuit missionary is indispensable for any study of Patagonia. It is the first Spanish translation of the *Description of Patagonia and the Adjoining Parts of South America.* Hereford, 1774.

436. Hawksworth, John, ed. *An Account of the Voyages Undertaken by the Order of H.M., for Making Discoveries in the Southern Hemisphere, and Successfully Performed by Commodore Byron, Cap. Wallis, Cap. Carteret, and Cap. Cook.* 4 vols. London, 1773; Paris, 1774.

437. Menéndez, Fray Francisco. *Viajes de Fray Francisco Menéndez a la cordillera.* Publicados y comentados por Francisco Fonck. Valparaíso, 1896.

   The account of the expedition of 1783-84 in search of a convenient pass over the Cordillera south of Chiloé I.

438. ——. *Viajes de Fray Francisco Menéndez a Nahuel-huapi.* Publicados y comentados por Francisco Fonck. Valparaiso, 1900.

The account of the expedition in search of the lake and the fabled city of "los Césares," 1790-91.

439. Nodal, Bartholome Garcia de. *Relación del viage, que por orden de Su Magestad, y acuerdo de la Real Consejo de Indias, hicieron los capitanes Bartholome Garcia de Nodal, y Gonzalo de Nodal, hermanos, naturales de Pontevdra. al descubrimiento del Estrecho de San Vicente, que hoy es nombrado de Maire, y reconocimiento de Magallanes.* Madrid and Cadiz: D. Manuel Espinosa de los Monteros, 1766 or 1769.

The account of the voyage of the Nodal brothers, who made the first circumnavigation of Tierra del Fuego. Contains sailing instructions and an excellent description of the Fuegans.

b. Secondary sources.

440. Caillet-Bois, Ricardo R. "Las Islas Malvinas." *Historia de la Nación Argentina.* Edited by the Junta de Historia y Numismática Americana, Ricardo Levene, Dir.-Gen. Buenos Aires: Imprenta de la Universidad, 1950, Vol. 7, Pt. 2, Ch. V, pp. 369-414.

A good, brief historical sketch of the Malvinas or Falkland Islands.

441. Menéndez, Raúl. "Esquema del Descubrimiento de América del Sur." *Revista Geográfica Americana,* 16 (Buenos Aires, Octubre 1941): 238-51.

442. Moreno, Juan Carlos. *Nuestras Malvinas y La Antártida, Viaje de estudio y observación.* 5a. ed. Buenos Aires: Junta de Recuperacion de las Malvinas, 1949.

Contains a brief history of the Malvinas Is.

443. Rubio, Julián Maria. *Exploración y conquista del*

Río de Plata, siglos XVI y XVII. 8ª, ed. (Tomo VIII, Historia de América y de los pueblos americanos.) Dirigida por Antonio Ballesteros y Beretta. Barcelona and Buenos Aires: Salvat Editores, S.A., 1942.

A thorough, scholarly account. Very useful.

C. The Missionary explorers.

1. Primary sources.

444. Fernández, Juan Patricio. *Relación historical de las misiones de Indios Chiquitos que en Paraguay tienen los padres de la Compañía de Jesús.* 2 vols. Colección de libros raros o curiosos que tratan de América. Vols. 12-13. Madrid: Librería de Victoriano Suárez, Editor, 1895. (The two volumes were published separately in Asunción in 1896.)

A very useful account of the Jesuit missionaries in the province of Paraguay, and their exploring activities, by one of the missionaries.

445. Figueroa, Francisco de. *Relación de las misiones de la Compañía de Jesús en el país de los Maynas.* Madrid: 1904.

By one of the early explorers of the upper Amazon. Original title: *Ynforme de las misiones de el Marañón, Gran Pará, e Río de las Amazonas.*

446. Fritz, Samuel. *Journal of the Travels and Labours of Father Samuel Fritz in the River of the Amazons between 1686 and 1723.* London: The Hakluyt Society, 1922.

The journal of the Bohemian Jesuit who explored almost the entire length of the Amazon. A first-rate, most interesting account. This edition contains two maps, one a reproduction of Father Fritz's.

447. Grillet, Jean, and François Bechamel. *A Journal of the Travels of John Grillet and Francis Bechamel into Guiana in the Year 1674, in Order to Discover the Great Lake of Parima and the Many Cities Said to be Situated on its Banks, and Reputed the*

Richest in the World. London: Samuel Buckley, 1698.

A most interesting narrative of the experiences of two French Jesuits in exploring Guiana, and of their failure to find the fabled Lake Parima.

448. Jesuits--Letters from missions. *La Argentina vista por viajeros del siglo XVIII.* Buenos Aires: Editorial Huarpes, 1946.

A brief but useful collection.

449. Jesuits--Letters from Missions. *Cartas avulsas (1550-68).* Rio de Janeiro: Imprenta Nacional, 1887. (Reprinted, Rio de Janeiro: Officina Industrial Graphica, 1931.)

A valuable collection of letters from the Brazilian missions.

450. Jesuits. *Cartas edificantes y curiosas, escritas de las misiones estrangeras y de Levante por algunos misioneros de la Compañia de Jesús.* 16 vols. Madrid: 1753-57. (Also published as *Lettres édificantes et curieuses,* Vols. 1-2 in 1, Paris: 1702-3 and *Letters from the Missions,* 14 vols., Paris: 1829.)

An extensive collection including letters from Jesuit missions all over the world. The American missions are covered in the last volumes.

451. Jesuits. *Voyages et travaux des missionaires de la Compagnie de Jésus publiés par des pères de la même Compagnie pour servir de complément aux Lettres Édificantes.* I. Mission de Cayenne et de la Guyana Française. Paris: 1857.

This volume includes narratives of the major voyages, plus a list and brief description of voyages into the interior after 1674.

452. Jiménez de la Espada, Marcos, ed. *Noticias auténticas del famoso rio Marañón y misión apostólica de la Compañia de Jesús de la provincia de Quito en los dilatados bosques de dicho rio.* Madrid: 1889.

A good collection of reports from the Amazon missions of the Jesuits.

2. Secondary sources.

453. Arcila Robledo, Gregorio. *Las misiones franciscanas en Colombia; estudio documental.* Bogota: Imprenta Nacional, 1950.

    A well-documented, scholarly work, especially good on the Amazon missions, pp. 281-384.

454. Azevedo, João Lúcio d'. *História de Antônio Vieira com factos e documentos novos.* 2 vols. Lisboa: 1918.

    A detailed and very useful narrative of the life and travels of the great Jesuit missionary in Brazil.

455. ———. *Os jesuítas no Grão-Pará, suas missões e a colonizacão.* 2a ed. rev. Coimbra: Imprensa da Universidade, 1930.

    A very useful account by a Portuguese scholar; the best book on the subject.

456. Barros, André de. *Vida do padre Antônio Vieira.* Lisboa: J.M.C. Seabra & T.Q. Antunes, 1858.

    A valuable biography by an eighteenth-century historian.

457. Borda, José Joaquín. *Historia de la Compañía de Jesús en la Nueva Granada.* 2 vols. Poissy: 1872.

    A good survey of Jesuit activity in Colombia.

458. Brazil, São Paulo. Comisáo Nacional para as Comemoracões do "Dia de Anchieta." *Anchietana.* São Paulo: Secretária de Educacão e Cultura, 1965.

    An excellent collection of papers, monographs, etc. on Padre Anchieta, one of the great Jesuit missionaries in Brazil.

459. Demontézon, Fortuné, ed. *Mission de Cayenne et de la Guyane française.* Paris: Julien, Lanier, Cosnard, 1857.

   A good history of the missions in French Guiana.

460. Espinosa Gómez, Carlos. "El bosquerón del Padre Abad." *Boletín de la Sociedad Geográfica de Lima,* 79 (Sept.-Dic. 1962): 26-37.

   A brief narrative of the journey of Fray Matías Abad, a Franciscan missionary, in the forests of New Granada.

461. Fúrlong Cárdiff, Guillermo. *Cartografía jesuítica del Río de la Plata.* Buenos Aires: Talleres s.a. Casa Jacobo Peuser ltda., 1936.

   An excellent study, containing superb maps.

462. ———. *Entre los abipones del Chaco; según noticias de los misioneros jesuítas, Martín Dobrizhoffer, Domingo Muriel, José Brigniel, Joaquín Camaño, José Jolís, Pedro Juan Andreu, Jose Cardiel y Vicente Olcina.* Buenos Aires: Talleres Gráficos "San Pablo," 1938.

463. Henriques Leal, António. *Apontamentos para a história dos jesuitas no Brasil extrahídos dos chronistas da companhia de Jesus.* Rio de Janeiro: J. Leite e cia., 1871.

464. Izaguirre Ispizua, Bernardino. *Historia de las misiones franciscanas y narración de los progresos de la geografía en el oriente del Perú; relatos originales y produciones en lenguas indígenas de váríos misioneros ... 1619-1921.* 14 vols. in 13. Lima: Tipográficos de la Penitenciaría, 1922-29.

   A very useful history of the missions operated by the Franciscans in Peru, based on original narratives reprinted in the series. There are useful maps and tables.

465. Jouanen, José, S.J. *Historia de la Compañía de Jesús en la antigua Provincia de Quinto.* 2 vols. Quinto: Editorial Ecuatoriana, 1941-45.

The definitive study; volume 1 covers from 1570 to 1696, volume 2 continues to 1778.

466. Leite, Serafim. *História da Companhia de Jesus no Brasil*. 10 vols. Lisboa: Livraria Portugalia, 1938-50.

    A work of great scholarship; the definitive study. The first three volumes cover the great age of missionary-explorers.

467. Lodares, Baltasar de. *Los franciscanos capuchinos en Venezuela*. 3 vols. Caracas: 1929-30.

    Of interest primarily for a brief account of the expedition of 1720-21 in search of El Dorado.

468. Mulhall, Mrs. Marion (McMurrough). *Explorers in the New World Before and After Columbus and the Story of the Jesuit Missions of Paraguay*. London and New York: Longmans, Green & Co., 1909.

469. Pôrto, Aurelio. *História das missões orientais do Uruguai*. Vols. 1- . Rio De Janeiro: Imprensa Nacional, 1943- .

470. Restrepo, Daniel, S.J. *La Compañís de Jesús en Colombia*. Bogotá: Imprenta del Corazón de Jesús, 1940.

    A good, standard account.

471. Rippy, J. Fred, and Jean Thomas Nelson. *Crusaders of the Jungle*. Chapel Hill: University of North Carolina Press, 1936.

    An excellent, scholarly, sympathetic study.

472. Rivero, Juan. *Historia de las misiones de los llanos de Casanare y los rios Orinoco y Meta*. Bogotá: Empresa Nacional de Publicaciones, 1956.

    By an eighteenth-century missionay-explorer. Contains valuable geographical and scientific information.

473. Santos García, Brother. *La geografía del oriente peruano y los jesuitas*. Lima: Imprenta Torres Aguirre, 1945.

Seventeenth- and Eighteenth-Century Exploration 87

A brief account of Jesuit contributions to the geographical knowledge of eastern Peru.

474. Severn, Derk. "A Missionary on the Amazon, 1686-1724: Fr. Samuel Fritz." *History Today*, 25 (Apr. 1975): 279-86.

475. Ybot-León, Antonio. *La iglesia y los eclesiásticos españoles en la empresa de Indias*. 2 vols. Barcelona: Salvat, 1954 and 1963.

A valuable, lengthy, scholarly account.

D. Scientific exploration.

1. Primary sources.

476. Aguirre, Juan Francisco. "Diario de Aguirre." Biblioteca Nacional *Anales*, 4 (Buenos Aires, 1905): ix-xi; 7 (1911).

The diary of his work on the Spanish-Portuguese boundary commission in the Parana region, 1777.

477. Alvear y Ponce de León, Diego de. "Diario de la segunda partida demarcadora de límites en la América Meridional; por su comisario Don Diego de Alvear, 1783-1971." Biblioteca Nacional *Anales*, 1 (1900):195-384; 2 (1902):288-360; 3 (1904):373-464.

The diary is edited from a MS. in the Biblioteca Nacional, Buenos Aires, by Paul Groussac.

478. Azara, Félix de. *Descripción e historia del Paraguay y del Río de la Plata*.... 2 vols. Madrid: Imprenta de Sánchez, 1847. Asunción: A. de Uribe y cia., 1896. Buenos Aires: Editorial Bajel, 1943.

By the head of the Spanish boundary commission in Paraguay, who spent twenty years in South America.

479. _____. *Diario de la navegación y reconocimiento del río Tebicuarí*. Buenos Aires: Imprenta del Estado, 1836.

A brief narrative of the exploration of this river while the author was head of the Spanish boundary commission in Paraguay in the late 18th century.

480. _____. *Geografía física y esférica de las provincias del Paraguay, y misiones guaraníes*. Bibliography, prologue and notes by Rodolfo Schuller. Montevideo: Talleres A. Barreiro y ramos, 1904.

    Contains a lengthy prologue, with maps, plans, and a table. The MS. is in the Biblioteca Nacional in Montevideo.

481. _____. *Viajes inéditos de D. Félix de Azara desde Santa-Fe á la Asunción, al interior del Paraguay, y a los pueblos de misiones con una noticia preliminar por el General D. Bartolomé Mitre y algunas notas por el doctor D. Juan Marta Gutiérrez*. Buenos Aires: Imprenta y Librería de Mayo, 1873.

    Personal accounts by this head of the boundary commission turned explorer and naturalist.

482. _____. *Voyages dans l'Amérique méridionale dépuis 1781 jusqu'en 1801*. 4 vols. and atlas. Paris: Dentu, 1809. (Spanish translation as *Viajes por la América del Sur*, with notes by Cuvier. 2 vols. in 1. Montevideo, C.A. Walekenaer, 1845-46. Also Madrid: Espasa-Calpe, 1923.)

    A valuable, descriptive account by a member of the boundary commission.

483. *Charts and Plates to La Pérouse's Voyage*. London: G.G. & J. Robinson, 1798.

    Contains 32 plates, including an engraving of La Pérouse, and a map of the voyage (Plate 3). See Items 492, 493, and 494.

484. Cook, James. *The Journals of Captain James Cook on His Voyages of Discovery*. Edited by John C. Beaglehole. 3 vols. Cambridge: The Hakluyt Society, 1955-61.

    An excellent edition with a superb introduction.

485. Córdoba Lazo de la Vega, Antonio de. *Relación del último viaje al estrecho de Magallanes de la fragata de S.M. Santa María de la Cabeza, en los años 1785 y 1786.* Madrid: 1787. (English translation as Cordova, Don A. de. *A Voyage of Discovery to the Strait of Magellan: With an account of the Manners and Customs of the Inhabitants; and of the natural productions of Patagonia....* London: n.d.)

   The report of a 3-month scientific mission which produced an excellent map of the Strait and a complete descriptive navigation track.

486. Courte de la Blanchardière, René. *Nouveau voyage fait au Pérou.* Paris: Imprimerie de Delaguette, 1751.

   An interesting first-hand account of a voyage to Peru by way of Tierra del Fuego, by a French priest. Rare.

487. *Diario de la segunda división de límites al mando de D. Diego de Alvear, teniente de navío de la real armada, con la descripción de su viage desde Buenos Aires para reconocer los terrenos neutrales entre el Chuy y Tahín, el Río Grande de San Pedro, y la laguna Merín con todos sus verteres.* (Colección Relativa a la Historia del Río de la Plata, Vol. 4.) Buenos Aires: Imprenta del Estado, 1837.

   A brief narrative, of interest primarily for its very good description of these remote regions.

488. Ferreira, Alexandre Rodregues. "Diario de viagem philosophica pela Capitania de São-José do Rio-Negro com a informação do estado presente." *Revista Trimensal do Instituto Histórico Geográphico e Ethnográphico do Brasil,* 48 (1885): Parte 1, 1-234; 51 (1888): 5-166.

   The journal of a naturalist.

489. Feuillée, Louis, *Journal des observations physiques, mathématiques, et botaniques.* Paris: Pierre Giffart, 1714.

An interesting, useful narrative of early scientific exploration along the coasts of Chile and Peru.

490. Frézier, Amadée François. *A Voyage to the South-Sea, and along the coasts of Chili and Peru in the Years 1712, 1713, and 1714.... Postscript by Dr. Edmund Halley ... and an Account of the Settlement, Commerce, and Riches of the Jesuits in Paraguay.* London: Jonah Bower, 1717.

Especially valuable for contemporary maps and excellent illustrations, thirty-seven in number.

491. Froger, François. *Relation d'un voyage de la mer du Sud, detroit de Magellan, Brésil, Cayenne, et las isles Antilles.* Amsterdam: l'Honoré et Chatelain, 1715.

A rare and valuable account of the expedition of Jean-Baptiste de Gennes which set out in 1695 to found a colony in the Strait of Magellan, written by one of its members. Contains some excellent engravings.

492. Haenke, Thaddaeus Perigrinus. *Descripcion del Reyno de Chile.* Introduccion de Augustín Edwards. Santiago: Nascimiento, 1942.

Based on his explorations as a member of the Malaspina expedition and after.

493. ———. "Memoria sobre los rios navegables que fluyen al Marañon, procedentes de las cordilleras del Perú y Bolivia." *Coleccion de documentos literarios del Peru,* Vol. 2. Edited by Manuel de Odriozola. Lima, 1863-77.

494. ———. *Viaje par el virreinato del Río de la Plata.* Buenos Aires: Emecé Editores, s.a., 1943.

Contains some plates illustrating the journey.

495. La Condamine, Charles-Marie de. *A Succinct Abridgement of a Voyage Made Within the Inland Parts of South-America.* London: E. Withers, 1747. (Trans. of *Relation abrégée d'un voyage fait dans l'intérieur de l'Amérique méridionale.* Paris,

1745; the entire narrative appears in *Journal du voyage fait par l'ordre du roi à l'équateur.* Paris, 1747.)

The narrative of the expedition sent to Quito to measure an arc of longitude near the Equator. A very useful abridgment of this indispensable work, entirely satisfactory for nearly all purposes.

496. Lapérouse, Jean-Francois de Galaup, comte de. *Le voyage de Lapérouse sur les côtes de l'Asie et Californie (1786) avec une introduction et les notes par Gilbert Chinard.* Baltimore: Johns Hopkins University Press, 1937.

While this extract from the official account (see Item 503) does not deal with South America, the introduction is useful.

497. _____. *The First French Expedition to California. Lapérouse in 1786.* Trans., intro., and notes by Charles N. Rudkin. Los Angeles: Glen Dawson, 1959.

This is a translation only of Chs. X, XI and XII of the official account (see Item 503), but the introduction is of some value.

498. _____. *Voyages and Adventures of La Pérouse.* Trans. by Julius S. Gassner. Honolulu: University of Hawaii Press, 1969.

A good, accurate translation, condensed from the 14th edition of the original account.

499. Malaspina, Alessandro. *Letters of D. Alexandro Malaspina.* Collected and edited by William Inglis Morse. Boston: McIver Johnson Co., 1944.

Contains facsimiles and maps.

500. _____. *Viaje al río de la Plata en el siglo XVIII; reedición de los documentos relativos al viaje de las corbetas Descubierta y Atrevida e informes de sus oficiales sobre el virreinato, estraídos de la obra de Novo y Colson* ....Buenos Aires: Librería y editorial "La Faculdad," Bernabé y cia., 1938.

Half the volume covers preparations and the voyage; the remainder includes scientific notes and appendices.

501. _____. *Tablas de latitudes y longitudes de los principales puntas del Río de las Plata, nuevamente arreglados al meridiano que pasa por lo mas occidental de la isla de Ferro.* Buenos Aires: Imprenta del Estado, 1837.

    The result of surveys made while exploring the Río de la Plata.

502. _____. *Viaje político-científico alrededor del mundo por las corbetas Descubierta y Atrevida al mando de los capitanes de navío d. Alejandro Malaspina y don José de Bustamente y Guerra desde 1789 á 1794, publicado con un introducción por don Pedro de Novo y Colson.* Madrid: Imprenta de la Viuda e Hijos de Abenzo, 1865.

    The full account of Malaspina's voyage, with tables and maps.

503. Milet de Moreau, Louis-Marie-Antoine Destouff, Baron de. *Voyage de La Pérouse autour du monde.* 3 vols. Paris: Imprimerie Nationale, 1797.

    The official, unabridged account of Lapérouse's ill-fated voyage around the world.

504. Ovando-Sanz, Guillermo, ed. *Tadeo Haenke: Su obra en los Andes y la selva boliviana.* La Paz: Editorial Los Amigos del Libro, 1974.

    A collection of seven of Haeke's essays on Bolivia. A list of his unpublished MSS, his published books, and books about him appears in the bibliography.

505. Ruiz, Hipólito. *Relación del viaje hecho a los reynos del Perú y Chile por los botánicos y dibuxantes enviados para aquella expedición, extractado de los diarios por el orden que llevó en estos su autor.* Rev. by R.P. A.J. Barreiro, O.S.A. Madrid: Est. Tipográfico Huelves y Compañía, 1931.

A very detailed, technical account of the journey. Very useful.

506. _____. *Travels of Ruiz, Pavón, and Dombey in Peru and Chile (1777-1788), with an Epilogue and Official Documents Added by Agustín Jesús Barreiro.* Trans. by B.E. Dahlgren. (Vol. 21 in Botanical Series, Field Museum of Natural History.) Chicago: Field Museum, 1940.

    A useful, briefer version of the *Relación* (Item 505).

507. Taillemite, Etienne. *Bougainville et ses compagnons de voyage autour du monde, 1766-1769.* 2 vols. Paris: Imprimerie Nationale, 1978.

    A collection of documents, including Bougainville's journal and accounts by six others. The lengthy introduction describes preparations, the ships, the participants, techniques, scientific findings, and contemporary reactions.

508. Ulloa, Antonio de, and Jorge Juan y Santacilia. *Relación histórica del viage a la América meridional hecho de orden de Su Magestad.* 4 vols. Madrid: Antonia Maria, 1748. (English trans. by John Adams, with notes, as A *Voyage to South America.* 2 vols. London: Lockyer Davis, 1772.)

    Another English edition, published by Stockdale in London in 1808, contains a dedicatory note to Commodore Home Popham in honor of his capture of Buenos Aires, "that Territory which now is, and will most probably remain, from your Foresight, Ability, and personal Bravery, one of the riches Jewels in the United Crown." This is a work of detailed and careful observation.

509. Viana, Francisco Javier de. *Diario del viage explorador de las corbetas españolas "Descubierta" y "Atrevida."* Cerrito de la Victoria, Imprenta del Ejército, 1849.

    The narrative of the Malaspina expedition. A useful firsthand account.

2. Secondary sources.

510. Arias Divito, Juan Carlos. "Expediciones científicos españoles al Nuevo Mundo." *Nuestra Historia*, 10 (Dec. 1971): 195-201.

   A brief but useful survey, covering primarily the eighteenth century.

511. Ballivián, Manuel Vicente, and Pedro Kramer. *Tadeo Haenke*. Escritos precedidos de algunos apuntes para su Biografía y acompañados de various Documentos Illustrativos. La Paz: El Nacional, 1898.

   A valuable study by one of Bolivia's leading scientists.

512. Beaglehole, John C. *The Life of Captain James Cook*. Stanford: Stanford University Press, 1974.

   An outstanding account of Cook's voyages. This lengthy book gives little information about Cook's personal life, concentrating on his work as one of the greatest navigators and explorers of all time.

513. Erickson, Robert F. "The French Academy of Sciences Expedition to Spanish America, 1735-1744." Ph.D Dissertation, University of Illinois, 1955. 16/03, p. 523. BFJ00-15202.

   A thorough, well-researched study of the La Condamine expedition.

514. Ferreira Reis, Arthur Cezar. "A viagem filosofica e as expedicoes cientificas na Ibero-America no seculo XVIII." *Cultura* (Rio de Janeiro, Dic. 1952): 94-103.

   A brief, highly useful article on scientific exploration.

515. Forero, Manuel José. "Las expediciones botánicas de la Nueva Granada y de la Nueva España." *Boletín de Historia y Antigüedades*, 61 (Bogotá, 1974): 144-52.

   A brief but useful introduction to the botanical expeditions.

516. Guillot Muñoz, Alvaro. *La vida y obra de Félix de Azara: un sabio formado en el desierto.* Buenos Aires: Atlantida, S.A., 1941.

    The first 63 pages of this brief (156 pp.) work are devoted to Azara's life and work; the remainder consists of excerpts from his writings.

517. Novo y Colson, Pedro de. *Viaje científico ... por las corbetas Descubierta y Atrevida, al mando del Capitán D. Alejandro Malaspina.* Madrid: 1885.

    The definitive work on the subject, very well-documented.

518. Parodi, Lorenzo R. "Thaddeus Perigrinus Haenke a dos siglos de su nacimiento." *Anales de la Academia Nacional de Ciencias Exactas, Físicas, y Naturales de Buenos Aires,* 17 (1964): 9-13.

    A brief but valuable article, containing portraits of Malaspina and Haenke, and a map.

519. Parramore, Thomas C. "Anson's Voyage and the Dawn of Scientific Navigation." Ph.D. Dissertation, University of North Carolina, 1965. 26/07 p. 3912. BFJ65-14379.

520. Ponce Sanguiñes, Carlos. *Tadeo Haenke y su viaje a Samaipata en 1795.* La Paz: Centro de Investigaciones Arqueológicas, 1794.

    A brief study of one of Haenke's expeditions in Bolivia.

521. Ratto, Héctor R. *La expedición de Malaspina.* Buenos Aires: 1945.

    Based entirely on Malaspina's own account.

522. Tafur Garcés, L. "Exploraciones y expediciones científicas a territorios grancolombianos (Hoyas del Orinoco, Amazonas, Guayas, Atrato y Magdalena)." *Boletín de Historia y Antigüedades,* 42 (Bogotá, 1955): 167-80.

    A good, succinct introduction to the subject.

523. Torre Revello, José. *Los Artistas Pintres de la expedición Malaspina*. (Universidad de Buenos Aires, Instituto de Investigaciones Históricas, Estudios y Documentos para la Historia del Arte Colonial, Vol. 2. Buenos Aires: Universidad de Buenos Aires, 1944.

    Contains the best paintings of the expedition. There is a good introduction and an extensive bibliography.

524. Valentin, François. *Voyages et aventures de Lapérouse*. 3. éd. Tours: A. Mame, 1872.

525. Whitaker, Arthur P. "Antonio de Ulloa." *Hispanic American Historical Review*, 15 (1935): 155-94.

    The only study of Ulloa available in English. A work of excellent scholarship.

VII. NINETEENTH- AND TWENTIETH-CENTURY EXPLORATION

A. Nineteenth-century exploration in general.

1. Primary sources.

526. Agassiz, Alexander. *Letters and Recollections of Alexander Agassiz.* Ed. by G.R. Agassiz. Cambridge: University Press, 1913.

His expeditions into Peru, Chile, California, Mexico, Panama, and the Galápagos Islands. He was the son of the great naturalist, Louis Agassiz.

527. Baldrich, Juan Amadeo. *Las comarcas vírgines; el Chaco Central norte.* Buenos Aires: J. Penser, 1889.

Describes his explorations in the Río Pilcomayo region; includes studies of soil hydrography, climate, Indians, ethnography, and the flora and fauna.

528. Brand, Charles (Lt., R.N.) *Journal of a Voyage to Peru: a Passage Across the Cordillera of the Andes, in the Winter of 1827, Performed on Foot in the Snow, and a Journey Across the Pampas.* London: Hesson Colburn, 1828.

A most interesting first-hand account of his journey. There are four illustrations.

529. Bresson, André. *Sept années d'explorations, de voyages, et de séjours dans l'Amérique Australe.* Préface de M. Ferdinand de Lesseps. Paris: 1886.

A good description of Chile and Peru with numerous documents on the Hispanic American republics.

530. Brisson, Jorge. *Casanare*. Bogotá: Imprenta Nacional, 1896.

531. Bürger, Otto. *Reisen eines Naturforschers im Tropischen Amerika*. Leipzig: T. Weicher, 1900.

   Deals primarily with Colombia.

532. Burmeister, Hermann. *Reise durch die La Platastaaten, mit besonderer rücksicht auf die physiche beschaffenheit und die culturzustrand der Argentinischen republik. Ausgeführt in die jahren 1857, 1858, 1959, und 1860*. Halle: H.W. Schmidt, 1861. (Translated into Spanish as *Viaje por los estados del Plata, con referencia especial a la constitución física y al estado del cultura de la República argentina realizado en los años 1857, 1858, 1859, y 1860*. Buenos Aires: Unión Germánica en la Argentina, 1933-34. 3 vols.)

   The journal of an eminent zoölogist, who was also a careful observer of all around him.

533. ———. *Reise nach Brasilien, durch die provinzen von Rio de Janeiro und Minas Geraës. Mit besonderer rücksicht auf die naturgeschichte der gold- und diamantendistricte*.... Berlin: Druck und Verlag von G. Reimer, 1853. (Translated into Portuguese by Manuel Salvaterra and Hubert Schoenfeldt as *Viagem ao Brasil, através des províncias do Rio de Janeiro e Minas Gerais, visando especialmente a história natural dos distritos auri-diamantíferas*. São Paulo: Livraria Martins, 1952.)

534. Burton, Richard F. *Exploration of the Highlands of Brazil*. 2 vols. London: Tinsley Bros., 1869.

   Volume 2, covering the Rio São Francisco journey, is the most useful. The Appendix is a translation of an old MS. reporting the discovery of a lost city in 1753.

535. Chaffanjon, Jean. *L'Orénoque et la Caura; relation de voyages exécutés en 1886 et 1887*. Paris: Hachette & Cie, 1889.

Describes the indigenous Indians and their language as well as the rivers.

536. Chikhachev, Platon Alexandrovich. *A Trip across the Pampas of Buenos Aires (1836-1837)*. Translated by Jack Weiner. Lawrence, Kansas; Center of Latin American Studies, University of Kansas (Occasional Publications No. 8, May 1967).

(Translated from Weiner's English translation of the Russian by Magdalena García Pinto as "Viaje a través de las pampas de Buenos Aires." *Boletín del Instituto de Historia Argentina*, 9 (No. 14-15, Buenos Aires, 1967): 14-106.)

A delightful, interesting account of the journey of a Russian aristocrat east across the Andes and the pampas from Santiago. Reconstructed largely from memory after his notes and documents were stolen from his hotel room in Paris.

537. ———. "Vision de Chile en los tiempos del Presidente Prieto (1837)." *Boletín de la Academia Chilena de Historia*, 34 (77) (Santiago, 2º sem. 1967): 206-12.

* Church, George Earl. *Explorations Made in the Valley of the River Madeira from 1764 to 1868*. London: National Bolivian Navigation Co., 1875.

Same as Item 409. An account of extensive explorations in the north of Bolivia.

538. Cochrane, Charles Stuart (Capt., R.N.). *Journal of a Residence and Travels in Colombia During the Years 1823 and 1824*. 2 vols. London: Henry Colburn, 1825.

A very interesting narrative of his experiences in Colombia.

539. Conway, William Martin, Baron of Allington. *The Bolivian Andes: a Record of Climbing and Exploration in the Cordillera Real in the Years 1898 and 1900*.... New York and London: Harler & Bros., 1901.

The explorations of an English art historian and explorer who began his career as a mountain climber at the age of 16. He climbed Mt. Illimani in 1898.

540. Coudreau, Henri Anatole. "L'Amazonia." *Société de Géographie Commerciale de Paris, Bulletin*, 8 (Paris: 1886): 122-64.

A brief summary of his Amazon explorations. Coudreau was a French historian, geographer, and ethnographer who began exploring South America, particularly Amazonia and Guiana, in 1882. After 1895 and until his death in 1899 he was in the service of the government of the State of Pará; these explorations are listed under the heading "Scientific Exploration, 19th Century: State Sponsored."

541. ———. *Explorations en Guyane*. Rouen: Cagniard, 1892.

Deals chiefly with explorations on the Oyapok River.

542. ———. *La France Equinoxiale*. 2 ed. 2 vols. Paris: Challamel Ainé, 1886-87.

A long narrative of his travels and explorations in Guyand and Amazonia. There is an accompanying atlas.

543. ———. *Voyage au Rio Branco, aux montagnes de la lune, au haut Trombetta, mai-1884-avril-1885*. Rouen: Cagniard, 1886.

Extract from the *Bulletin de la Société Normande de Géographie*.

544. Cruz, Luis de la. *Viage, a su costa, del alcalde provincial del muy ilustre cabildo de la Concepción de Chile D. Luis de la Crus, desde el Fuerte de Ballener ... hasta la Ciudad de Buenos Aires....* Buenos Aires: Imprenta del Estado, 1835.

545. Ehrenreich, Paul Max Alexander. *Viagem do Paraguay no Amazonas. A segunda expedição alemã ao rio Xingú. Viagens nos rios Amazonas e Purús.* (Tr. by by Alexandre Humad.) Sao Paulo: "Diario Official," 1929.

The expedition discovered the sources of several tributaries of the Amazon, including the Tocantins.

546. Fitz Gerald, Edward Arthur. *The Highest Andes*. Metuchen, N.J., 1899.

   A very useful work. The purpose of the expedition was the triangulation and ascent of Mt. Aconcagua. The enterprise was successful, although altitude sickness prevented Fitz Gerald from reaching the summit himself.

547. Fonseca, João Severiano da. *Viagem ao rededor do Brasil*. 2 vols. Rio de Janeiro: Typ. de Pinheiro & Co. 1880-81. Deals primarily with explorations in Mato Grosso. There are illustrations and a map.

548. Garcés, Modesto. *Un viaje a Venezuela*. Bogotá, 1890. An account of explorations made in 1885.

549. Gerstäcker, Fiedrich Wilhelm Christian. *Adventures in the Tropics*. Tr. by F.L. Oswald. New York: W.L. Allison, 1898.

   A well-written narrative of the experiences of this well-traveled German in South America.

550. _____.*Gerstäcker's Travels. Rio de Janeiro, Buenos Ayres, Ride Through the Pampas, Winter Journey Across the Cordilleras, Chili, Valparaíso, California and the Gold-Fields*. London and Edinburgh: T. Nelson & Sons, 1854.

551. _____. *Narrative of a Journey Round the World, Comprising a Winter Passage Across the Andes to Chile, with a Visit to the Gold Regions of California and Australia, the South Sea Islands, Java, etc*. London: Hurst & Blackett, 1853. 3 vols.

552. _____. *Neue Reisen durch die Vereinigten Staaten, Mexiko, Ecuador, Westindien, und Venezuela*. Jena: Costenoble, 1868-69. 3 vols.

   Volume 3 deals with South America.

553. _____. *Reisen ... neu durchgesehen und herausgegeben von Dietrich Theden*. 4th ed. Jena: Costenoble, n.d. 2 vols. Volume 1 is pertinent.

554. Hettner, Alfred. *Die Anden des westlichen Colombiens.* n.p., 1893.

> The explorations of a German geographer, professor at Leipzig, Tübingen, and Heidelberg.

555. ———. *Die Kordillere von Bogotá.* Gotha: J. Peythas.

> Explorations dealing with the physical geography of the region. There are maps and profiles.

556. ———. *Reisen in den colombianischen Anden.* Leipzig: Drucker & Humbolt, 1888.

557. Kappler, August. *Holländisch-Guiana. Erlebnisse und erfahrungen während eines 43 jährigen aufenhatts in der kolonie Surinam.* Stuttgart: W. Kohlahammer, 1881.

> Narrative of his life as a naturalist, 1842-46, and on the Maroni River, 1846-79.

558. Karsten, Hermann. *Florae Columbiae terrarumque adiacentium specimina selecta in peregrinatione duodecim annorum observata delineavit et descripsit H. Karsten.* 2 vols. Berolini: F. Duenamlerum Redemptorem, 1959-69.

> The results of Karsten's long study of the flora of Colombia. The text is in Latin and German.

559. ——— (sole author). *Informe sobre la especidión esploradora del Río Corcovado en los Andes patagonicos* .... Santiago: Imprenta Nacional, 1895.

560. ——— (sole author). *Mitteilungen uber den verlauf und die ergebnisse der Palena-expedition ...* Santiago: Druckerei Cervantes, 1895.

> Contains a map of the areas explored.

561. Krüger, Paul, and Paul Stange. *Informe preliminar sobre la espedición esploradora de los ríos Reñihué i Ftaleufu en la Patagonia occidental....* Santiago : Imprenta Nacional, 1897.

A brief introduction to their work in Patagonia.

562. Lista, Ramón. *Exploracion de la costa oriental de la Patagonia.* Buenos Aires, 1880.

    A brief account of explorations in the years 1876-79.

563. _____. *Mis esploraciones y descubrimientos en la Patagonia, 1877-80.* Buenos Aires: Imprenta de M. Biedma, 1880. Contains illustrations and maps of value.

564. _____. *El territorio de las Misiones.* Buenos Aires: Imprenta "La Universidad" de J.L. Klingelfuss, 1883.

565. _____. *Viaje al país de los Tehuelches: exploraciones en la Patagoia austral.* Buenos Aires, Imp. de M. Biedma, 1879.

566. Magalli, Joseph, ed. *Voyage d'exploration d'un missionaire dominicain chez les tribus sauvages de l'Equateur.* Paris, Bureaux de l'Année Dominicaine, 1889.

    An excellent, interesting narrative on the work of Father Pierre.

567. Markham, Clements R. "On the Supposed Sources of the River Purus, one of the Principal Tributaries of the Amazon." *Journal of the Royal Geographical Society,* 25 (1855): 151-58.

    By the great British geographer and authority on Peru.

568. _____. *Travels in Peru and India.* London: Murray, 1862.

    Expeditions in search of chinchona plants.

569. Maw, Henry Lister. *Journal of a Passage from the Pacific to the Atlantic, Crossing the Andes in the Northern Provinces of Peru and Descending the River Marañon or Amazon.* London: Murray, 1829.

    A very readable and entertaining account.

570. Middendorf, Ernst. *Peru. Beobachten und Studien über das Land und seine Bewohner während eines 25 jährigen Aufenhalte.* 3 vols. Berlin: R. Oppenheim, 1893-95. (Spanish translation as *El Perú.* Arequipa: J.I. de Olazabal, 1924.)

571. Monnier, Marcel. *Des Andes au Para.* Paris: Plon, 1890.

    Contains some very good maps.

572. Muñoz, David. *Memorias de viaje y datos relativos a los salvajes de la region oriental....* Lima: Imprenta de la Escuela de Ingenieros, 1901.

    A brief account by a Peruvian priest with useful data on the Indians.

573. O'Connor d'Arlach, Tomás. *De los Andes al Plata.* La Paz: González y Medina, 1914.

    The work of a Bolivian novelist-turned-explorer.

574. Osculati, Gaetano. *Esplorizione delle regione equatoriali luego il Napo ed il fiume delle Amazzone.* Milano: Tip. Bernardoni, 1850.

575. Parish, Woodbine. "Account of a Voyage to Explore the River Negro from its Mouth on the East Coast of South America to its Supposed Sources in the Cordillera of Chile." *Journal of the Royal Geographical Society,* 6 (1836): 136-67.

576. Pavie, Théodore. *Fragments d'un voyage dans l'Amérique méridionale en 1833.* Angers: Imp. de V. Pavie, 1840.

    The author was a widely-traveled orientalist.

577. Peabody, George Augustus. *South American Journals (1858-1859).* Edited from the original MS. by John Charles Phillips. Salem, Mass.: Peabody Museum, 1937.

    His journey to Brazil, Uruguay, Argentina, Chile, and Peru. There is a good description of the Pacific coast.

578. Plane, Auguste. *A Travers l'Amérique Equatoriale. Le Pérou.* Paris, 1903.

Various explorations into the interior of Peru. There are two maps and 23 plates.

579. Pons, François Raymond Joseph de. *Travels in South America.* London: R. Phillips, 1806. (Appears as No. 2 in Richard Phillips, *A Collection of Modern and Contemporary Voyages and Travels*, Vol. 4.) An abridgement of his *Voyage to the Eastern Part of Terra Firma*.... Item 580. Contains a useful map of the Captaincy-General of Caracas.

580. ———. *A Voyage to the Eastern Part of Terra Firme, or the Spanish Main, in South-America During the Years 1801, 1802, 1803, 1804*.... New York: I. Riley & Co., 1806. (Translated from the French in part by Washington Irving.)

Pons was an agent of the French government at Caracas. He gathered information of all aspects of life in the Captaincy-General--topography, commerce, agriculture, population, the Church, geography, political affairs, etc. The sections on the Indians, his journey up the Orinoco River, and speculations as to its source are of particular interest.

581. Quijarro, Antonio. *Exploraciones efectuadas en el Río Madre de Dios y sus afluentes.* La Paz: Imprenta El Comercio, 1890.

The work of a Bolivian who explored this remote part of his country extensively.

582. Raimondi, Antonio. *Notas de viajes para su obra "El Perú.* Lima: Imprenta Torres Aguirre, 1942- Vols. 1- .

The work of a native of Milano, who went to Peru in 1850 to become his adopted country's greatest explorer. He explored the Cordillera, Tarapacá, Cuzco, the valley of the Urubamba river, the Huallaga, Marañón, and Ucayali rivers, Huaraz, and Lake Titicaca. (See also Item 603.)

583. Regel, Fritz (Christian Friedrich Leopold). *Kolumbien*. Berlin: A. Schall, 1899.

   The work of a German geographer who explored Antioquia extensively in 1896-97. Well-illustrated, with a map.

584. Saint-Cricq, Laurent. *Travels in South America from the Pacific Ocean to the Atlantic Ocean....* New York: Scribner, Armstrong, 1875. 2 vols.

   Contains 525 wood engravings by E. Rion and 10 maps from drawings by the author.

585. Sievers, Wilhelm. *Geografía de Bolivia y Perú*: traducción del alemán por Carlos de Salas. Barcelona and Buenos Aires: Editorial Labow, S.A., 1931.

   The work of a German geographer, who explored in Venezuela, Ecuador, and Peru in the latter part of the nineteenth century.

586. ———. *Reise in der Sierra Nevada de Santa Marta*. Leipzig: Gressner & Schramm, 1887.

587. Simson, Alfred. *Travels in the Wilds of Ecuador and the Exploration of the Putamayo River*. London: Sampson, Low, Marston, Searle & Rivington, 1886.

   A good account of a journey into the eastern part of Ecuador and what is now Peru.

588. Smyth, William, and Frederick Lowe. *Narrative of a Journey from Lima to Para across the Andes and down the Amazon*. London: John Murray, 1836.

   The narrative of two British naval officers who made the journey to investigate the feasibility of the Amazon route as an outlet for the products of the interior.

589. Squier, Ephraim George. *Peru, Incidents of Travel and Exploration in the Land of the Incas*. New York: Harpers, 1877.

   A valuable account of archeological exploration. This book provided the inspiration for Thornton Wilder

Nineteenth- and Twentieth-Century Exploration

(*The Bridge of San Luis Rey*) and for Hiram Bigham's subsequent explorations in the twentieth century.

590. Steinmann, Gustav. *Geologie von Peru*. Heidelberg: C. Winter, 1929.

    The work of a German geologist and paleontologist who explored in Peru, Bolivia, Argentina and Chile.

591. Stephens, Henry. *Journeys and Experiences in Argentina, Paraguay, and Chile Including a Side Trip to the Source of the Paraguay River in the State of Matto Grosso in Brazil and a Journey across to the Rio Tambo in Peru*. 2nd ed. New York: Knickerbocker Press, 1920.

592. Stübel, Alfons. *Die ruinenstätte von Tiahuanaco im hoch lands des alten Perú; eine kulturgeschichtliche studie auf grand selbstaendiger aufnahmen*.... Breslau: Verlag von C.T. Wiskott, 1892.

    By a German geologist and vulcanologist who explored Peru, Ecuador, and Colombia between 1868 and 1878.

593. Thouar, Arthur. *Explorations dans l'Amérique du Sud*. Paris: Hachette et c^{ie}m 1891.

    The narrative of an expedition ordered by the French government to seek the survivors of the ill-fated Crevaux expedition. A very interesting account, with numerous illustrations and maps.

594. Whymper, Edward. " A Journey among the Great Andes of the Equator." *Proceedings of the Royal Geographical Society* (New Series, London: Edward Stanford, 1881): 449-71.

    A well-written brief summary of the experiences of one of England's greatest mountaineers in Ecuador.

595. ――――. *Travels amongst the Great Andes of the Equator*. 2nd ed. London: J. Murray, 1892.

    A solid, lengthy account of his experiences in climbing the peaks, including Cotopaxi and Chimborazo, with extensive botanical information.

596. Wied-Neuwied, Maximilian, Prince of. *Reise nach Brasilien in den Jahren 1815 bis 1817.* 2 vols. Frankfurt-am-Main: Bronner, 1820-21.

    This intensive study of the Botocudos Indians was the first truly scientific monograph about a Brazilian tribe.

2. Secondary sources.

597. Barbosa de Oliveira, Américo. "Considerações sobre a exploração da castanha no baixo e médio Tocantins." *Revista Brasileira de Geografia.* (Jan. 1940): 3-15.

* Church, George Earl, comp. *Explorations Made in the Valley of the River Madeira from 1764 to 1868.* London: National Bolivian Navigaiton Co., 1875.

    Item 408.

598. Habel, Jean. *Ansichten aus Südamerika.* Berlin: Verlag von Dietrich Reimer, 1897.

599. Oberacker, Carlos. "Viajantes, Naturalistas e Artistas." *História Geral da Civilizacão Brasileira.* Edited by Sérgio Buarque de Holanda. São Paulo: Difusão Européia do Livro, 1962. Vol. 3, Ch. 5, 119-31.

    An excellent, concise survey of their work. Compare Pinto (Item 601) and Schaden and Pereira (Item 603).

600. Ojeda, V.A. "La region oriental y sus vías de penetración." *Miscelanea* (Quito, Agos. 1934): 23-36.

601. Pinto, Olivério M. Oliveira. "Viajantes a naturalistas." *História Geral da Civilização Brasileira.* Edited by Sérgio Buarque de Holanda. São Paulo: Difusão Européia do Livro, 1967. Vol. 5, Ch. 7, 425-47.

    A concise, valuable essay on the subject. Compare Oberacker (Item 599) and Schaden and Pereira (Item 603).

602. Raimondi, Antonio. *El Perú; itinerarios de viajes (versión literal de las libretas originales)....*

Lima: Imprenta Torres Aguirre, 1929.

A chronological list of explorations, edited by the greatest explorer of Peru. Part three covers the 19th century.

603. Schaden, Egon, and João Baptista Borges Pereira. "Exploração antropólogica." *História Geral da Civilização Brasileira.* Edited by Sérgio Buarque de Holanda. São Paulo: Difusão Européia do Livro, 1967. Vol. 5, Ch. 6, 406-24.

 A valuable, well-written essay. Complements Oberaker (Item 599) and Pinto (Item 601).

B. The great naturalists.

 1. Primary sources.

604. Adalbert, Prince of Prussia. *Travels of H.R.H. Prince Adalbert of Prussia.* 2 vols. London: D. Bogue, 1849.

 The Prince conducted extensive explorations along the Rio Xingu.

605. Appun, Karl Ferdinand. *Unter den Tropen. Wanderungen durch Venezuela am Orinoco durch Britisch Guyana und am Amazonenstrome in den jahren 1849-68.* Jena: H. Costenoble, 1871. 2 vols. (Translated by Federica de Ritter as *En los trópicos.* Caracas: Universidad Central de Venezuela, Ediciones de la Biblioteca, 1961.)

 A lively, fascinating account by a German naturalist who spent twenty years in Venezuela.

606. Bates, Henry Wallace. *The Naturalist on the River Amazons.* London, 1863. Reprinted, Berkeley and Los Angeles: The University of California Press, 1962.

 One of the most interesting and pleasing of all the works written by the explorers. Bates spent many years along the Amazon collecting insects, some of them in the company of Alfred Russel Wallace.

607. Darwin, Charles. *Charles Darwin's Diary of the Voyage of H.M.S. "Beagle."* Edited from the MS. by Nora Barlow. Cambridge: The University Press, 1933.

This excellent edition of Darwin's narrative is one of several available to the reader. It delineates his explorations in South America, the results of which first suggested to him the idea of evolution.

608. _____. *Journal of Researches into the Natural History and Geology of the Countries Visited during the Voyage of H.M.S. Beagle Round the World, under the Command of Capt. Fitz Roy, R.N.* New York: Appleton, 1884.

609. _____. *Life and Letters of Charles Darwin, Including an autobiographical chapter.* Edited by his son Francis Darwin. 3 vols. London, 1887.

Includes letters to his friends and to his critics; valuable for the insight they give into his character.

610. Edwards, William H. *A Voyage up the River Amazon, Including a Residence at Para.* New York: D. Appleton & Co., 1847; London: John Murray, 1847.

A valuable work not only for its content but also for the fact that Edwards was the first American naturalist to write about South America.

611. Gauss, Carl Friedrich. *Briefe zwischen Alexander von Humboldt und Gauss, herausgegeben von K. Bruhns.* Leipzig, 1877.

Letters between Humboldt and the celebrated German mathematician and astronomer Gauss, valuable for their descriptive matter.

612. Hirsch, Lina. "Viagem do Príncipe Paulo Alexandre de Wuerttemberg." *Revista do Instituto Histórico e Geográfico Brasileiro*, 171 (1936): 6-30.

Translation of a notebook of a German naturalist's journey.

613. Humboldt, Alexander von. *Aspects of Nature, in*

Different Lands and Different Climates; with Scientific Elucidations. Trans. by Mrs. Sabine. Philadelphia: Lea & Blanchard, 1849.

Contains some valuable information on his South American explorations.

614. ―――. *Briefe an seinen Bruder. Herausgegeben von der Familie von Humboldt in Ottmachau.* Stuttgart, 1880.

Contains valuable descriptive material on South America. Written to his brother Wilhelm.

615. ―――. "Cartas de Alejandro Humboldt sobre su estada en el Perù." *Boletín de la Biblioteca Nacional,* 49-50 (Lima, 1969): 7-19.

616. ―――. *Essai sur la géographie des plantes.* Paris: Levrault, Scheoll et cie., 1805. Reprinted, London: Society for the Bibliography of Natural History (Sherborn Fund Facsimile No. 1), 1959.

A paper read at the class of physical and mathematical sciences at the National Institute in Paris, 1805.

617. ―――. *Examen critique de l'Histoire de la Géographie du nouveau continent et des progrès de l'astronomie nautique aux quinzième et seizieme siècles.* Paris: Librairie de Gide, 1836-39. 5 vols.

Of value chiefly in showing Humboldt's concepts of the historical geography of the New World.

618. ―――. *A Geognostical Essay on the Superposition of Rocks in Both Hemispheres.* Trans. from the French. London: Longmans, 1823.

The results of his geological studies in South America.

619. ―――. *Lettres américaines d'Alexandre de Humboldt (1787-1807). Précédés d'une Notice de J.-C. Delametherie et suivies d'un choix de documents en*

partie inédits. Publiées avec une introduction et des notes par De. E.T. Hamy. Paris: Librairie Orientale et Américaine, 1905.

Humboldt's letters written from America. Indispensable for any study of his explorations in South America.

620. _____. *Memoria rezonada de las salinas de Zipiquirá.* Bogotá, 1888.

621. _____. *Personal Narrative of Travels to the Equinoctial Regions of the New Continent during the Years 1799-1804.* English trans. from the French by Helen Maria Williams. 5 vols. Philadelphia: M. Carey, 1815.

This is an excellent translation of one of the greatest travel narratives. A superb account in every respect. It covers his explorations as far as Nueva Granada (modern Colombia), and must be supplemented by his *Researches* (Item 622) and *Views of Nature* (Item 623), which complete the narrative to Peru.

622. _____. *Researches Concerning the Institutions and Mounments of the Ancient Inhabitants of America.* London: Longmans, 1814. 2 vols.

Describes some of his experiences and researches in Peru.

623. _____. *Views of Nature: or Contemplations on the Sublime Phenomena of Creation.* Trans. from the German by E.C. Otté and H.G. Bohn. London: George Bell & Sons, 1878.

Reflections on his South American experiences.

624. _____, and Aimé Bonpland. *Monographie des melastomacées.* Mise en ordre par A. Bonpland. Paris: Chez Gide Fils, 1830.

A folio volume containing beautiful plates, their colors still vivid, of a certain family of trees found by Humboldt and Bonpland in South America.

625. Im Thurn, Everard. *Among the Indians of Guiana.* London: K. Paul, Trench & Co., 1883.

   The work of a British ornithologist, who finally dispelled the Lake Parima myth.

626. _____. "The Ascent of Mount Roraima." *Proceedings of the Royal Geographical Society,* 7 (New Series, London: Edward Stanford, 1885): 497-521.

   The story of the first ascent of this not unusually high mountain, long believed to be unclimbable.

627. Kerr, John Graham. *A Naturalist in the Gran Chaco.* Cambridge: University Press, 1950.

   The author was Regius Professor of Zoölogy at the University of Glasgow. The work covers the Río Pilcomayo expedition of 1889-91 and the expedition in search of the Lepidosiren fish, an early type of vertebrate.

628. Poeppig, Eduard Friedrich. *Reise in Chile, Peru, und auf dem Amazonen Ströme während der Jahre, 1827-32.* Leipzig: F. Fleischer, 1835-36. 2 vols. in 1. Stuttgart: Brockhaus, 1960.

   His experiences in the Andes, and his botanizing expeditions into the *montaña* of Peru. The Leipzig edition contains some musical scores for Andean music; the Stuttgart edition contains a great number of excellent plates.

629. Posada, Eduardo. "Cartas de Humboldt." *Boletín de Historia y Antigüedades,* 50 (Nov. 1907): 65-84.

   Letters written in Colombia and Peru to Bolívar and Restrepo, and from them to Humboldt.

630. Saint-Hilaire, Augustin François César Prouvençal de. "Aperçu d'un voyage dans l'intérieur du Brésil, la province Cisplatine et les missions dites du Paraguay." *Mémoires du Museum d'Histoire Naturelle,* 9 (Paris, 1822): 307-80. Also printed separately, Paris: Impr. de A. Berlin, 1823.

   A paper read at the Académie des Sciences. Saint-

Hilaire was an eminent French naturalist who labored many years in Brazil.

631. ———. "Esquisse de mes voyages au Brésil et Paraguay." (Introduction to his *Histoire des plantes ... du Brésil et du Paraguay*, Item 632.) No. 1 in Vol. 10, *Chronica Botanica*. Waltham, Mass.: 1946.

632. ———. *Histoire des plantes les plus remarquables du Brésil et du Paraguay*. Paris: A. Belin, 1824.

The results of many years, botanizing in Brazil and Paraguay.

633. ———. *Segunda viagem ao interior do Brasil, Espíritu Santo, traducção de Carlos Madeira*. São Paulo: Companhia Editora Nacional, 1936. (*Bibliotheca pedagogica brasileira*. Ser. 5^a: Brasiliana. Vol. 71, i.e., 72.)

634. ———. *Segunda viagem do Rio de Janeiro a Minas Geraes e a São Paulo, 1822*. Trans. by Afonso d'Escragnolle Taunay. São Paulo: Cia. Editora Nacional, 1932. (New edition: revised translation and preface by Vivaldi Moreira, notes by Mário G. Ferri. São Paulo and Belo Horizonte: Editora da Universidade de São Paulo, Itatiaie, 1974.)

635. ———. *Viagem à Comana de Curitiba* (1820). Trans. by Carlos da Costa Pereira. São Paulo: Cia. Editora Nacional, 1964.

636. ———. *Viagem ao Espíritú Santo e Rio Doce*. Trans. by Milton Amado, preface by Mário Guimarães Ferri. São Paulo and Belo Horizonte: Editora da Universidade de São Paulo, Itatiaia, 1974.

637. ———. *Viagem ao Rio Grande do Sul (1820-1821)*. Trans. by Leonora de Azevedo Penna. São Pualo and Belo Horizonte: Editora da Universidade de São Paulo, Itatiaia, 1974.

638. ———. *Viagem as nascentes do Rio S. Francisco, e pela província de Goyaz*. Trans. and notes

by Claudio Ribeiro de Lessa. São Paulo: Cia. Editora Nacional, 1937. 2 vols.

639. ———. *Viagem no interior do Brasil (quarta parte) relativa ao atual estado do Paraná.* Trans. by David A. da Silva Carneiro. Curitiba: J.B. Groff, 1931.

640. ———. *Viagem pelas províncias de Rio de Janeiro e Minas Gerais.* Trans. and notes by Claudio Ribeiro de Lessa. São Paulo: Cia. Editora Nacional, 1938. 2 vols.

641. ———. *Voyages dans l'interieur du Brésil.* Paris: Gimbert et Dorez (1 ptie.), Libraire-Gide (2 ptie.), A. Bertrand (3-4 ptie.), 1830-51. 8 vols. in 4.

The original complete French edition of the explorations and travels of this celebrated French botanist; the result of careful, exacting research.

642. Smith, Herbert H. *Brazil: the Amazons and the Coast.* New York: Charles Scribner's Sons, 1879.

The work of an American naturalist, who explored most of the major regions of Brazil between 1868 and 1874; he was attracted by the great variety of flora and fauna in that country.

643. Spruce, Richard. *Notes of a Botanist on the Amazon and Andes.* 2 viks, London: Macmillan, 1908.

A valuable source, the story of his eventful explorations along the Amazon. Edited and condensed by Alfred Russel Wallace.

644. Stuart, (Henry Windsor) Villiers. *Adventures amidst the Equatorial Forests and Rivers of South America.* London: J. Murray, 1891.

The work of an ornithologist. Contains 21 plates.

645. Tschudi, Johann Jakob von. *Die brasilianische provinz Minas Gerais.* Gotha: J. Perthes, 1862.

Written by Tschudi from the original letters of the engineers on the exploring expedition.

646. ———. *Reise durch die Andes von Süd-Amerika von Cordova nach Cobija im jahre 1858.* Gotha: J. Perthes, 1860.

A brief (38 pp.) account of this journey.

647. ———. *Reisen durch Süd-Amerika.* Leipzig: Brockhaus, 1866-69. 5 vols.

There are numerous illustrations and maps. Volumes 1 and 2 are concerned with his explorations into the interior of Brazil, volume 3 with the southeastern coastal states, volume 4 with the south of Brazil and Rosario in Argentina, and volume 5 with northern Argentina, Chile and Peru.

648. ———. *Travels in Peru during the Years 1838-42, 1854.* London: D. Bogue, 1947.

Tschudi was the first European in some of the areas he visited. The translation from the German by Thomasina Ross is somewhat faulty.

649. Wallace, Alfred Russel. "On the Rio Negro." *Journal of the Royal Geographical Society,* 23 (1853): 212-17.

There is a good map on pp. 212-213.

650. ———. *A Narrative of Travels on the Amazon and Rio Negro....* London: Ward, Locke & Co., 1889.

His account of extensive explorations in the Amazon region, partly in the company of Bates.

651. ———. *Travels on the Amazon.* London: Ward, Locke & Co., 1911.

A new edition of Item 650, corrected and enlarged.

652. Wassermann, Felix M. "Six Unpublished Letters of Alexander von Humboldt to Thomas Jefferson." *The Germanic Review,* 29 (1954): 191-201.

653. Waterton, Charles. *Wanderings in South America.* London: Dent; New York: Dutton, 1895.

　　This delightful book, detailing the explorations of one of the early naturalists in South America, has gone into several editions despite the author's apology for it.

2. Secondary sources.

654. Acosta Solís, Misael. "La ascensión de Humboldt al Chimborazo." *Anales de la Universidad de Cuenca,* 25 (3) (Jul.-Set. 1969): 47-50.

655. Arias de Grieff, Jorge. "Itinerario de Humboldt y Bonpland." *Boletín de la Sociedad Geográfica de Colombia,* 26 (100) (1968): 253-58.

　　The journey from Cartagena to Santa Fe de Bogotá, Popayán, and Pasto, based on MS. materials.

656. ―――. "El Mapa del Río Magdalena de Humboldt." *Boletín Cultural y Bibliográfico,* 13 (1) (Columbia, 1970): 46-48.

　　The 1801 map reproduced is one of four copies of the original, which has not been found.

657. Banse, Ewald. *Alexander von Humboldt, Erschliesser einer neuen Welt.* Stuttgart, 1953.

　　Written by a professional geographer in the Humboldt tradition. Contains many hitherto unpublished documents. Describes Humboldt as the last universal scientist before the age of specialization.

658. Beck, Hanno. *Alexander von Humboldt.* 2 vols., Wiesbaden: 1959-61.

　　A magnificent biography, based in part on new material from documents not used before, factual and accurate. It is the first long biography since that of Karl Bruhns in 1873 (Item 661).

659. Berrill, N.J. "Electric Fishes." *Natural History,* 62 (Dec. 1953): 450-55.

Contains material from Humboldt's *Personal Narrative* (Item 621) on this subject.

660. Botting, Douglas. *Humboldt and the Cosmos*. New York: Harper & Row, 1973.

    The most recent shorter biography of Humboldt, well-done and very useful for a good presentation of his work.

661. Bruhns, Karl C. *Life of Alexander von Humboldt*. 2 vols. London: 1873.

    The first good long biography of Humboldt, a classic in its field.

662. "Centenary of Humboldt's Journey." *Harper's Weekly*, 48 (April 16, 1904): 577-83.

663. Chardón, Carlos Eugenio. *Los naturalistas en la América latina*. Ciudad Trujillo: Editores del Caribe, 1949.

    The first volume of a projected multi-volume work. It covers the 16th through the 18th centuries, and includes Humboldt and Darwin as well.

664. Crone, G.R. "Alexander von Humboldt: Centenary Studies." *Geographical Journal*, 127 (1962-63): 226-27.

665. Cutright, Paul Russell. *The Great Naturalists Explore South America*. New York: Macmillan, 1940.

    Part I, pp. 3-46, is historical; the remainder consists of descriptions of specific fauna. There are good brief biographical sketches.

666. De Terra, Helmut. "Alexander von Humboldt's Centenary." *Science*, 127 (March 21, 1978): 635-48.

    Information concerning planned celebrations, and the gathering of Humboldt documents in libraries.

667. ———. *Humboldt: the Life and Times of Alexander von Humboldt, 1769-1859*. New York: Knopf, 1955.

A first-rate biography, based on excellent primary sources, by a geologist.

668. Dojcsak, G.V. "Alexander von Humboldt." *Canadian Geographical Journal*, 81 (1970): 33-37.

Covers his scientific work in South America.

669. García, Rodolpho. "História das explorações scientíficas." Instituto Histórico e Geográfico Brasileiro, *Diccionario histórico, geográfico, e etnográfico do Brasil*, I, 856-910. Rio de Janeiro: 1922.

Concerned chiefly with the naturalists.

670. Gendron, Val. *The Dragon Tree. A Life of Alexander, Baron von Humboldt*. New York and London: Longmans, 1961.

A detailed work of careful research, intended for young people, but of value for anyone interested in science. Contains an outline of Humboldt's five-volume *Kosmos*.

671. Gómez, Picón, Rafael. "El barón Alejandro de Humboldt y su presencia en América." *Boletín de Historia y Antigüedades*, 42 (Bogotá, Set.-Oct. 1955): 619-30.

Contains Bolivar's letters to Humboldt and his replies.

672. Hakspiel, Phil. "Alejandro de Humboldt en sus relaciones con Colombia y Venezuela." *Boletín de Historia y Antigüedades*, Año 8 No. 90 (Bogotá, 1912): 321-42.

Deals with Humboldt's impact on these countries subsequently.

673. Hammerly Dupuy, Daniel. "Alejandro de Humboldt y las exploraciones científicos en América." *Historia*, 16 (Buenos Aires, Abr.-Jun. 1959): 5-10.

A brief, interesting essay stressing the impact of his scientific work.

674. "Itinerario de Humboldt y Bonpland." *Boletín de la Sociedad Geográfica de Colombia*, 26 (100) (1968): 253-58.

Illustrated with a good map.

675. Kellner, Charlotte. *Alexander von Humboldt*. London: Oxford University Press, 1963.

A fine biography, based on excellent primary sources, by a physicist.

676. Klencke, Hermann. *Alexander von Humboldt; a Biographical Monument*. Trans. by Julietta Bauer. London: 1852.

An early biography, written during Humboldt's lifetime.

677. Macgillivary, W. *The Travels and Researches of Alexander von Humboldt*. New York: 1832.

One of the first studies of his explorations and scientific work.

678. Mattos, Anibal. *Peter Wilhelm Lund no Brasil. Problemas de paleontologia brasileira*. São Paulo: Cia. Editora Nacional, 1939.

The paleontological explorations of the great Danish archeologist.

679. McKinney, H(enry) Lewis. *Wallace and Natural Selection*. New Haven: Yale University Press, 1972.

A carefully-documented, fine piece of scholarship, presenting Wallace as an important naturalist.

680. Melón Ruíz de Gordajuela, Armando. "Humboldt en el conocer de España peninsular y Canarias." *Estudios Geográficos*, 18 (67-68) (Madrid, 1957): 239-59.

Provides background for Humboldt's American trip--his observations in Spain, obtaining permission to go, etc.

681. ———. "El viajero venezolano Francisco Michelena y Rojas, en pos y en contra de Humboldt." *Estudios Geográficos*, 1 (Madrid, Oct. 1940): 13-43.

   A comparison of the two journeys.

682. Meyer-Albich, A. *Alexander von Humboldt*. Bonn: Internationes, 1969.

   A good, recent biography by a Humboldt scholar.

683. ———. "The Hundredth Anniversary of the Death of Alexander von Humboldt." *Hispanic American Historical Review*, 38 (1958): 394-96.

684. Morales Macedo, Carlos. "Alejandro de Hunboldt." Academia Colombiana de Historia, *Conferencias*. Bogotá: 1946-47, 222-58.

   Good on the character and work of Humboldt.

685. Núñez, Estuardo. "América en la pasión de Humboldt." *Cuadernos Americanos*, 52 (Mexico, Jul. 1950): 169-82.

686. ———. "Retorno de Alejandro de Humboldt." *Boletín de la Biblioteca Nacional*, 49-50 (Lima, 1969): 3-6.

687. Pereyra, Carlos. *Humboldt en América*. Madrid: Editorial-América, 1917.

688. Peterson G., Georg. "La presencia de Alexander von Humboldt en el litoral del Perú." *Amaru*, 10 (1969): 2-10.

   A very good sketch of his journey along the coast of Peru, with a map. Cites works by Humboldt directly or indirectly related to Peru.

689. Rippy, J. Fred, and E.R. Brann. "Alexander von Humboldt and Simón Bolívar." *American Historical Review*, 52 (July 1947): 697-703.

690. Rocha, Levy. "Tschudi no Espírito Santo." *Revista do Instituto de História e Geografia Brasileiro*, 258 (Jan.-Mar. 1963): 11-16.

691. Schreibers, Karl von. "Noticias dos naturalistas imperiais austrácos no Brasil." *Revista do Instituto de História e Geografia Brasileiro*, 283 (Avr.-Jun. 1969): 191-254.

    The accomplishments of Johann Natterer and Johann Pohl, who came to Brazil in 1817.

692. Schwarzenberg. F.A. *Alexander von Humboldt, or What May Be Accomplished in a Life Time.* London: Robert Hardwicke, 1866.

    A good, somewhat brief biography written a few years after Humboldt's death.

693. Sinnhuber, Karl A. "Alexander von Humboldt." *Scottish Geographical Magazine*, 75 (1959): 89-101.

694. Sprague, T.A. "Humboldt's and Bonpland's Itinerary in Colombia." Royal Botanical Gardens, Kew, *Bulletin of Miscellaneous Information* (1926): 23-29.

695. ———. "Humboldt's and Bonpland's Itinerary in Mexico and Venezuela." Royal Botanical Gardens, Kew, *Bulletin of Miscellaneous Information* (1924): 20-27, (1925): 295-310.

696. Sternberg, S. von. "Pioneer of Science." *Popular Science Monthly*, 70 (April 1907): 292-95.

    A tribute to Humboldt.

697. Stoddard, Richard. *The Life, Travels, and Researches of Baron Humboldt.* London: 1859.

    Probably the first biography to appear in the year of Humboldt's death.

698. Stoetzer, Carlos O. "Alexander von Humboldt." *Américas*, 24 (Aug. 1972): 18-23.

    A brief, well-written biographical sketch with illustrations.

699. ———."Humboldt, a Hundred Years After." *Américas*, 11 (May 1959): 2-8.

700. Sylva, Rafel. "Fiat Lux." *Américas*, 27 (2)(1975): 17-24.

   Humboldt in Venezuela; the electric eel episode.

701. Verdoorn, Frans, ed. *Plants and Plant Science in Latin America*. Waltham, Mass.: Chronica Botanica Co., 1945.

   Covers every phase of botanical interest. There is a good "Historical Sketch" by F.W. Pennell, pp. 35-48.

702. Villiers, Alan. "In the Wake of Darwin's *Beagle*." *National Geographic*, 136 (Oct. 1969): 449-95.

   Villiers followed Darwin's course; an excellent article, well-written, with a map and numerous illustrations.

703. Von Hagen, Wictor Wolfgang, ed. *South America: The Green World of the Naturalists*. New York: Greenberg, 1948.

   Twenty-five selections from the writings of various naturalists, with footnotes and bibliography. A good collection.

704. ———. *South America Called Them*. New York: Knopf, 1945.

   A good, colorful, popular account based on primary sources and the author's own experiences. Includes La Condamine, Humboldt, Darwin, and Spruce.

705. Williams, Edward F. "Alexander von Humboldt." *Popular Science Monthly*, 80 (April 1912): 346-59.

   A short biography, with a description of his writings.

706. Woodcock, George. *Henry Walter Bates, Naturalist of the Amazons*. London: Faber & Faber, 1969.

   Covers Bates' work in the Amazon area from 1848 to 1859. There are numerous quotations from his papers, journals, and letters.

707. Zuloaga, Guillermo. "Humboldt in Venezuela." *Farol*, 31 (234)(Caracas, 1969): 5-13.

   A description of his journey, with a list of equipment.

C. Nineteenth-century scientific exploration: privately sponsored.

   1. Primary sources.

708. Agassiz, Louis. *His Life and Correspondence*. Ed. by Elizabeth Cary Agassiz. 2 vols., London: 1885.

   Invaluable for a study of the work of this great Swiss-American naturalist.

709. ―――, and Elizabeth Cary Agassiz. *A Journey in Brazil*. Boston: Ticknor and Fields, 1868. 3rd ed. (A Portuguese translation by Edgar S̈usskind de Mendonca appears as *Viagem ao Brasil, 1865-1866*. São Paulo: Cia. Editora Nacional, 1938.)

   The English version contains interesting woodcuts. The book describes explorations in the Amazon and the Rio de Janeiro area.

710. Antonina, *Barão de*. "Resumo do itinerario de uma viagem exploradora pelos rios Verde, Itarevê, Paranapanêma e seus affluentes, pelo Paraná, Ivechy, e sertões adjacentes, emprehendida por ordem de Ex. Sr. barão de Antonina." *Revista Trimensal de História e Geographia*, 9 (Rio de Janeiro, 1869): 17-42.

   A copy of the MS. giving a day-by-day account of this journey in 1845, signed by John Henrique Elliot.

711. ―――. "Itinerario das viagens exploradoras emprehendidas pelo Sr. barão de Antonina para descobrir uma via de communicação entre o porto da villa de Antonina e o Baixo-Paraguay na provincia de Mato-Grosso: feitas nos annos de 1844 a 1847 pelo sertanista o Sr. Joaquim Francisco Lopes, e descriptas pelo Sr. João Henrique Elliot." *Revista Trimensal de História e Geographia*, 10 (Rio de Janeiro, 1870): 153-77.

The unedited MS. of the journey submitted by Barao Antonina.

712. Boussingault, Jean-Baptiste Joseph Dieudonné. *Viajes científicos a los Andes ecuatoriales.* Paris: Librería Castellana, 1849.

    Strictly a series of scientific monographs concerning flora, fauna, resources, etc.

713. Bove, Giacomo. *Note di un viaggio nelle Missioni ed Alto Paraná, settembre 1884-febbraio 1885.* Genova: Tipografia del R. Istituto Sordo-Muti, 1885. Lucca: G. Giusti, 1923.

    Narrative of a journey sponsored by the Società Geografica Italiana, led by Bove, an eminent Italian explorer and veteran of the Arctic. He visited Patagonia and Tierra del Fuego, the Rio Iguaçú, and the upper Paraná.

714. ———. *Patagonia--Terra del Fuoco, mori australi. Rapporta ... al Comitato Centrale per la Esplorazioni Antartiche.* Parte I. Genova: Tip. del Real Istituto de'Sordo-Muti, 1883.

    This was the only part ever published.

715. ———. *Viaggio alla Patagonia ed alla Terra del Fuoco.* n.p., 1882.

716. Branner, John Casper. *Two Characteristic Geologic Sections on the Northeast Coast of Brazil.* Washington: The Academy, 1900.

    The results of the Branner-Agassiz expedition to Brazil.

717. Burckhardt, Carl Emanuel. *Rapport préliminaire sur une expédition géologique dans la région andine située entre Las Lajas (Argentine) et Curacautin (Chile) (38-39° latitude sud)....* La Plata: Talleres de Publicaciones del Museo, 1898.

718. Fontana, Luis Jorge. *Viaje de exploración en la Patagonia austral.* Buenos Aires: La Tribuna Nacional, 1886.

A report to the Minister of the Interior of explorations in the Chubut valley. Technically this was an officially-approved expedition, but all the funds were raised by a group of Welsh colonists who participated.

719. Hartt, Charles Frederick. *Geology and Physical Geography of Brazil*. Boston: Fields, Osgood & Co., 1870.

   The results of his explorations with the Thayer and Agassiz expeditions.

720. Moyano, Carlos M. *Viajes de exploración a la Patagonia, 1877-90*. Buenos Aires: 1931.

   An excellent, interesting account by one of Argentina's leading explorers.

721. Musters, George C. *At Home with the Patagonians*. London: J. Murray, 1973.

   A lively, most interesting narrative of his longitudinal journey through Patagonia.

722. ———. "A Year in Patagonia." *Journal of the Royal Geographical Society*, 41 (1871): 59-77.

   A brief summary of his Patagonian expedition.

723. Myers, Henry Morris. *Life and Nature Under the Tropics; or, Sketches of Travels among the Andes, and on the Orinoco, Rio Negro, and Amazonas*. New York: Appleton, 1871.

   The narrative of a scientific expedition from Williams College, 1867, led by James Orton. Brief on scientific aspects, already published by Orton.

724. Schomburgk, Moritz Richard. *Reisen in Britisch Guiana in den Jahren 1840-44*. 3 vols. Leipzig: J.J. Weber, 1847-48. (English translation of volumes 1 and 2 by Walter Roth as *Richard Schomburgk's Travels in British Guiana, 1840-44*. Georgetown, Br. Guiana: "Daily Chronicle, "1922-23. 2 vols.)

The story of his explorations in nearly every part of British Guiana; primarily an ethnographic and biological study. The maps in the English translation are inferior to those in the German edition.

725. Schomburgk, Robert H. "Diary of an Ascent of the River Corentyn in British Guiana in October 1836." *Journal of the Royal Geographical Society*, 1 (1837): 285-301.

726. ———. "Diary of an Ascent of the River Berbice in British Guiana in 1836-37." *Journal of the Royal Geographical Society*, 7 (1837): 302-350.

A map follows p. 350.

727. ———. "Expedition to the Lower Parts of the Barima and Guiania Rivers, in British Guiana." *Journal of the Royal Geographical Society*, 12 (1842): 169-78.

728. ———. "Excursions up the Barima and Cuyuni Rivers in British Guiana." *Journal of the Royal Geographical Society*, 12 (1842): 178-96.

729. ———. "Report of an Expedition into the Interior of British Guayana in 1835-36." *Journal of the Royal Geographical Society*, 6 (1836): 224-83.

A map appears on pp. 282-83.

730. ———. "Report of the Third Expedition into the Interior of Guayana, comprising the Journey to the Sources of the Essequibo, to the Carumá Mountains, and to Fort San Joaquin on the Rio Branco in 1837-38." *Journal of the Royal Geographical Society*, 10 (1841): 159-90.

731. ———. "Journey from Fort San Joaquin on the Rio Branco to Roraima, and thence to the rivers Parima and Mereweri to Esmeralda on the Orinoco in 1838-39." *Journal of the Royal Geographical Society*, 10 (1841): 191-247.

732. ———. "Journey from Esmeralda on the Orinoco to San Carlos and Moura on the Rio Negro, and thence by Fort San Jaoquin to Demerara, in the spring of

1839." *Journal of the Royal Geographical Society,* 10 (1841): 248-67.

733. ———. Robert Hermann Schomburgks *Reisen in Guiana und am Orinoko während der jahre 1835-39. Nach seinen berichten und mittheilungen an die Geographische Gesellschaft in London, hrsg. von O.A. Schomburgk.* Leipzig: G. Wigard, 1841.

> The complete account of his travels, illustrated, with a good map showing the route.

734. Steinen, Karl von den. *O Brasil Central. Expedição em 1884 para a exploração do Rio Xingu.* Tr. de Catarina Baratz Cannabrava. São Paulo: Editora Nacional, 1942.

> The exploration took place in the remote upper reaches of the Xingu, among tribes who had never seen a European.

735. ———. *Durch Central-Brasilien.* Leipzig: Brockhaus, 1886.

> The account of a more extensive exploration of the upper Xingu region, which considerably increased knowledge of the Indians of the area.

736. ———. *Entre os aborígines do Brasil Central.* Trans. by Egon Schaden. Preface by Herbert Baldus. São Paulo: Departamento de Cultura, 1940.

> Reprinted from the *Revista do Arquivo,* Nos. 34-58. There are illustrations, useful tables and maps, and a good preface.

737. ———. "O Rio Xingú." *Revista da Sociedade de Geographia do Rio de Janeiro,* 4 (1888): 189-212.

2. Secondary sources.

738. Amaya, Lorenzo. "La expedición Fontana a la Cordillera del Chubut (1885)." *Revista Geográfica Americana,* 4 (Oct. 1935): 255-69.

739. Leitão, Cândido Mello. *História das expedições científicas no Brasil.* São Paulo: Cia. Editora

Nacional, 1941. (Also appears in Instituto Histórico e Geográfico Brasileiro, Terceiro Congresso de História Nacional, Oct. 1938, *Anais*. Vol. 10, 217-500. Rio de Janeiro: Imprensa Nacional, 1944.)

A comprehensive study covering all areas of Brazil; includes botanical, zoölogical, and ethnographical expeditions. There is a useful index of names.

740. Mayano, María Clarisa. *Carlos Moyano, el explorador de la Patgonia*. Buenos Aires: Librería "El Ateneo" Editorial, 1948.

A good biography of this important explorer.

741. Núñez, Estuardo. "Los viajeros de tierra adentro, 1860-1900." *Journal of Inter-American Studies*, 2 (Jan. 1960): 9-44.

Covers the explorations of John Tucker, Louis and Alexander Agassiz, George Peabody, James Orton, and Adolphe Bandelier.

742. Rey Balmaceda, Alfredo. "El primer cruce longitudinal de la Patagonia." *Revista Geográfica Americana*, 39 (Mayo-Jun. 1955): 253-56.

Describes the expedition of George Chaworth Musters.

743. Rippy, J. Fred. *Latin America and the Industrial Age*. New York: G. Putnam's Sons, 1944, 1947.

Chapters 9 and 10 deal with Banner, Hartt et al. in Brazil.

744. Rocha, Levy. "Wied, Freyreiss, e Sellow no Espíritu Santo." *Revista do Instituto Histórico e Geográfico Brasileiro*, 297 (1972): 56-67.

745. Tafur Garcés, Leonardo. "Exploraciones y expediciones científicas a territorios grancolombianos (Hoyas del Orinoco, Amazonas, Guayas, Atrato y Magdalena)." *Boletín de Historia y Antigüedades*, 42 (Bogotá, 1955): 167-80.

A good introduction to the subject.

746. Torres, Ana Palese de. "Las exploraciones de Moyano en la Cuence del Santa Cruz." *Revista Geográfica Americana*, 38 (Buenos Aires, Dic. 1954): 124-28.

D. Nineteenth-century scientific exploration: government sponsored.

1. Primary sources.

747. Bertrand, Alejandro. *Memoria sobre las Cordilleras del desierto de Atacama i rejiones limítrofes, presentado al señor ministro del interior.* Santiago: Imprenta Nacional, 1885.

   Results of a geological expedition, 1884.

748. Bollaert, William. "Abstract of a Report made by Dr. R.A. Philippi to the Government of Chile, of a Journey into the Desert of Atacama in 1853-54." *Journal of the Royal Geographical Society*, 25 (1855): 158-71.

   Report of an extensive study of the desert made by a German scholar resident in Chile.

749. Brackenridge, Henry Maria. *Voyage to South America, Performed by Order of the American Government in the Years 1817 and 1818.* 2 vols. Baltimore: published by the author (John Toy, printer), 1819; London: T. & J. Allman, 1820; Spanish trans., Buenos Aires; 1927.

   A useful, informative account by the secretary of a trade commission sent to the Río de la Plata.

750. Brisson, Jorge. *Exploración en el alto Chocó.* Bogotá: Imprenta Nacional, 1895.

751. ———. *Viajes por Colombia en los años de 1891 a 1897.* Bogotá: Imprenta Nacional, 1899.

752. Castelnau, Francis de. *Expedition dans les parties centrales de l'Amérique du Sud.* Paris: P. Bertrand, 1850. 6 vols.

   The complete narrative of this expedition ordered

by the French government in 1843-47, with a folio supplement of illustrations. It includes expeditions in Brazil, Paraguay, Bolivia, Peru, the Gran Chaco, the Amazon area, and Guiana.

753. Codazzi, Giovanni Battista Agostino. *Memorie inedite di Agostino Codazzi, suoi viaggi per l' Europa e nelle Americhe (1816-1822)*. Milano: Edizioni "Alpes," 1930. (There is a recent Spanish translation as *Memorias de Agustín Codazzi* by Andrés Soriano Lleras and Alberto Lee López. Bogotá: Banco de la República, 1974.)

The extensive work of this Italian geographer in the service of the Republic of Gran Colombia. Both editions are well-illustrated with maps, engravings, etc., and both contain lengthy introductions with notes by Mario Longhena.

754. Coudreau, Henri Anatole. *Voyage à Itaboca et à l' Itacayuna, l^{er} juillet 1897-11 octobre 1897*. Paris: A. Lahure, 1898.

A voyage undertaken in the service of the State of Pará.

755. ———. *Voyage au Tapajoz, 28 juillet 1895-7 janvier 1896*. Paris: A. Lahure, 1897. (Portuguese translation by A. de Miranda Bastos, *Viagem ao Tapajós, 28 de julho de 1895-7 de janeiro de 1896*. São Paulo: Companhia Editora Nacional, 1897.)

An expedition in the service of the State of Pará to study the Indians and their languages, and to gather meteorological data. There is an excellent map of the Rio Tapajós.

756. ———. *Voyage au Tocantins-Araguaya, 31 décembre 1896-23 mai 1897*. Paris: A. Lahure, 1897.

In the service of the State of Pará. Lavishly illustrated, and contains a good map.

757. ———. *Voyage au Trombetas. 7 août 1899-25 novembre 1899*. Paris: A. Lahure, 1900.

In the service of the State of Pará. Actually

written by Mme O. Coudreau, second in charge. Coudreau died on this journey, 1899.

758. ———. *Voyage au Xingû, 30 mai 1896-26 octobre 1896.* Paris: A Lahure, 1897.

   In the service of the State of Pará. Includes a study of the Jurama and Arara Indians.

759. ———. *Voyage au Yamunda 21 janvier 1899-27 juin 1899.* Paris: A. Lahure, 1899.

   Contains 17 maps and a great number of illustrations.

760. ———. *Voyage entre Tocantins et Xingû 3 avril 1898-3 novembre 1898.* Paris: A. Lahure, 1899.

   In the service of the State of Pará. There are numerous illustrations and fifteen maps.

761. Coudreau, Mme O. *Voyage a la Mapuerá, 21 avril 1901-24 decembre 1901.* Paris: A. Lahure, 1903.

   In the service of the State of Pará. Well-illustrated.

762. ———. *Voyage au Canumã, 21 aoùt 1905-16 février 1906.* Paris: A. Lahure, 1906.

   While technically a twentieth-century expedition, this journey was a part of a long series under the sponsorship and direction of the State of Pará.

763. ———. *Voyage à Cuminá, 20 avril 1900-7 septembre 1900.* Paris: A. Lahure, 1901.

764. ———. *Voyage au Maycurú, 5 juin 1902-12 janvier 1903.* Paris: A. Lahure, 1903.

   A continuation of a series of explorations begun earlier under the sponsorship of the State of Pará. There are four maps and numerous illustrations.

765. ———. *Voyage au Rio Curuá, 20 novembre 1900-7 mars 1901.* Paris: A. Lahure, 1903.

766. Crawford, Robert. *Across the Pampas and the Andes*. London: Longmans, Green, 1884.

   The report of the chief engineer of the Transandine Railway Exploring and Surveying Expedition of 1871-72.

767. Crevaux, Jules Nicolas. *Voyages dans l'Amérique du Sud*. Paris: Hachette & Cie, 1883.

   The report of an expedition sent by the French Ministry of Public Instruction to explore the upper Paraguay River and reach the Amazon.

768. Expedición Austral Argentina. *Expedición austral argentina. Informes preliminares presentados a S.S.E.E. Los ministros del interior y de guerra y marina de la República Argentina por Giacomo Bove, jefe de la comisión científica de la expedición, y publicados bajo la dirección del Instituto Geográfico Argentino....* Buenos Aires: Imprenta del Departmento Nacional de Agricultura, 1883.

   The official account of this expedition to explore the south of Argentina, with a valuable introduction and documents relative to its work.

769. Fitz Roy, Robert, ed. *Narrative of the Surveying Voyage of His Majesty's Ships "Adventure" and "Beagle" between the Years 1826 and 1836*. 3 vols London: H. Colburn, 1839.

   By the captain of the *Beagle*; covers the exploration and survey of the southern coasts.

770. ———. "Extracts from the Diary of an Attempt to Ascend the River Santa Cruz in Patagonia, with the Boats of His Majesty's Sloop Beagle." *Journal of the Royal Geographical Society*, 26 (1857): 114-26.

   The article is followed by a map showing the route of the expedition.

771. France, Ministères de la Marine et de l'Instruction Publique. *Mission scientifique du Cap Horn, 1882-1883*. 6 vols. Paris: Gauthier-Villare, 1888.

   The official account. Very comprehensive.

772. Freycinet, Louis C. Desaules de. *Voyage autour du monde entrepris par ordre du Roi ... pendant les années 1817, 1818, 1819, et 1820.* 10 vols. Paris: 1824-44.

   The story of a French scientific expedition. Vol. 1, pp. 41-341 and Vol. 3, pp. 1348-80 deal with Brazil, primarily the region around Rio de Janeiro.

773. Giannéchini, Doroteo. *Diario de la Expedición exploradora Boliviana al Alto Paraguay de 1866 y 1887.* S.M. de Los Angeles: (Asís) Tip. de la Porciuncula, 1896.

774. Heath, Edwin R. *La exploración del Río Beni, revista histórica por el doctor Edwin R. Heath. Tr. y anotada por Manuel V. Ballivián.* La Paz: "La Revolución," 1896.

   The results of a scientific expedition under the auspices of the Ministerio de Instrucción Pública y Fomento.

775. Herndon, William L. *Exploration of the Valley of the Amazon. Under Direction of the Navy Department.* 2 vols. Washington: Robert Armstrong, 1853. New York: McGraw-Hill, 1952. (Abridged.)

   A most interesting and detailed account, well-written and containing much information.

776. Jiménez de la Espada, Marcos. *Diario de la expedición al Pacífico, llevada a cabo por una comisión de naturalistas durante los años 1862-1865.* Madrid: Imprenta del Patrono de Huérfanos de Intendencia e Intervención Militares, 1928.

   By an eminent Spanish zoölogist, member of the Spanish scientific expedition of 1862-65, which he describes.

777. ———. *El Iza o Putamayo.* Madrid, 1880.

   By a zoölogist on the 1862 Spanish expedition.

778. ———. "Noticias Auténticas del Famoso Río Marañón." *Boletín de la Scoiedad Geográfico de Madrid,* 27: 61-62.

779. ———. *El Río Putamayos y Marañón*. Madrid, 1890.

780. MacRae, Archibald. *Report of Journeys Across the Andes and Pampas of the Argentine Provinces.* (Vol. 2 of the *United States Naval Expedition to the Southern Hemisphere 1849-1852*, 3 vols.) Washington: A.O.P. Nicholson, 1856.

781. Michelena y Rojas, Francisco. *Exploración oficial por la primera vez desde el norte de la América del Sur siempre por ríos.... Viaje de Río de Janiero desde Belén en el Gran Pará por el Atlántico.* Brussels: A. Lacroix, 1867.

   Contains 7 maps. Useful to 1859.

782. Orbigny, Alcide D. d'. *Voyage dans Amérique méridionale éxécuté pendant les années 1826, 1827, 1828, 1829, 1830, 1831, 1832, et 1833.* 11 vols. Paris: Chez Pitois-Levrault et Cie., 1835-47.

   The comprehensive and definitive account of his early exploration, sponsored by the Museum d'Histoire Naturelle. His explorations included most of the southern part of the continent.

783. ———. *Voyage dans les deux Amériques*. Nouvelle ed. Paris: Furne, 1853.

   Supplements his *Voyage dans Amérique méridionale* (Item 782); covers his later travels.

784. Orton, James. *The Andes and the Amazon, or Across the Continent of South America.* New York: Harper & Bros., 1870.

   A very useful account of the Smithsonian Institution expedition.

785. Page, Thomas Jefferson. *La Plata, the Argentine Confederation, and Paraguay. Being a Narrative of the Exploration of the Tributaries of the River La Plata and Adjacent Countries during the Years 1853, '54, '55 and '56 under the Orders of the United States Government.* New York: Harper, 1859.

Lt. Page was the commander of this U.S. Navy expedition. There are illustrations, plates, tables, and a map, and an excellent account of the *Water Witch* incident.

786. Palacios, José Agustín. *Exploraciones de José Agustín Palacios realizados en los ríos Bení, Mamoré, Madeira y en el Lago Rogo-Aguado, durante los años 1844 al 47.* La Paz: Del Estado, 1944.

 The expedition was sent out by the Bolivian government to ascertain the navigability of these rivers.

787. Philippi, Rudolph Amand. *Viage al desierto de Atacama, hecho de orden del gobierno de Chile en el verano 1853-54.* Halle, Saxony: Eduard Anton, 1860.

 The author was professor of botany and zoology in the Instituto Nacional and director of the National Museum of Chile. The narrative was published under government auspices.

788. Pohl, Johann Baptist Emmanuel. *Reise in Innern von Brasilien ... in den Jahren 1817-21.* 2 vols., Wien, 1832-37. (Translated into Portuguese as *Viagem ao interior do Brasil emprendida nos anos de 1817 a 1821.* 2 vols. Rio de Janeiro: 1951.)

 Pohl was an Austrian physician, botanist, and mineralogist who went to Brazil with Spix and Martius.

789. Portillo, Pedro. *Las montañas de Ayacucho y los ríos Apurímac, Mantaro, Ene, Perené, Tambo, y alto Ucayali....* Lima: Imprenta del Estado, 1901.

 The journal of an official expedition, May-August 1900, to investigate the navigability of the rivers and the facilities for traffic of Ayacucho. Col. Portillo was prefect of the department of Ayacucho.

790. Reiss, Wilhelm and Alfons Stubel. *Reisen in Süd Amerika. Lepidepteren gesammelt auf einer reise durch Colombia, Ecuador, Perú, Brasilien, Argentinien und Bolivien in den jahren 1868-1877.* Berlin: Verlag von A. Ascher & Co., 1890.

The narrative of two geologists and mineralogists who accompanied the Wolf expedition (Item 810).

791. Schomburgk, Robert H. "Journal of an Expedition from Pirara to the Upper Corentyne, and from thence to Demerara, Executed by Order of Her Majesty's Government." *Journal of the Royal Geographical Society*, 15 (1845): 1-104.

The expedition was one of several to try to determine the boundary line between British Guiana and Venezuela; the result was known as the "Schmoburgk Line."

792. ———. "Visit to the Sources of the Takutu, in British Guiana, in the Year 1842." *Journal of the Royal Geographical Society*, 13 (1843): 18-75.

A report of part of the work undertaken by Schomburgk as a member of the Royal Boundary Commission.

793. Spix, Johann Baptist von, and C.F. Martius. *Travels in Brazil in the Years 1817-20. Undertaken by Order of H.M. the King of Bavaria.* 2 vols. in 1. London: Longman, Hurst, Reed, Orme, Brown & Green, 1824.

A valuable study of this expedition by members of the Academy of Sciences of Bavaria into the Amazon valley, with several good illustrations.

794. Steffen, Hans. *Informe sumario acerca del trascurso i resultados jenerales de la espedicion esploradora del río Cisnes*.... Santiago: Imprental Nacional, 1898.

A brief (30 pp.) report on this phase of the work of the Chilean-Argentine boundary commission.

795. ———. *Informe preliminar sobre la espedicion esploradora del río Aisen (diciembre 1896-abril 1897) presentado al señor ministro de relaciones esteriores, culto, i colonisacion.* Santiago: Imprenta Nacional, 1897.

A brief (28 pp.) report of part of the work of the Chilean-Argentine boundary Commission.

796. ———. "Nuevos aportes a la historia de la exploración de las cordilleras australes." *Revista Chilena de Historia y Geografía*, Set.-Dic. 1931: 150-81.

797. ———. *Reisen in den patagonischen Anden*. Berlin, 1900. His explorations in the Andes of Southern Chile.

798. ———. *Relación de un viaje de estudio a la rejión andina, comprendida entre el golfo de Reloncaví i el lago de Nahuelhuapi*.... Santiago: Imprenta Cervantes, 1892.

Part of the work of the Chilean-Argentine Boundary Commission.

799. ———. *Patagonia occidental, las cordilleras patagónicas y sus regiones circundantes; descripción del terreno basada en exploraciones proprias, con un bosquejo de la historia de las expediciones practicales en la región*. Traduc. de Julio González. 2 vols. Santiago: Universidad de Chile, 1944-48.

A very useful, comprehensive study with several maps, illustrations, and bibliographies at the end of each chapter.

800. ———. *Viajes de esploracion i estudio en la Patagonia occidental 1892-1902*. 2 vols. Santiago: Imprenta Cervantes, 1909.

A comprehensive study of exploration in Chilean Patagonia, with valuable maps.

801. ———. *Viajes i estudios en la rejion hidrográfica del rio Puelo (Patagonia occidental)*.... Santiago: Imprenta Cervantes, 1898.

Contains valuable appendices on the botanical geography of the Río Manso area, determination of altitudes, etc.

802. ———. *Westpatagonien. Die patagonischen Kordillera und ihre randgebiete*.... 2 vols. Berlin: D. Riemir, 1919.

803. Suárez Arana, Miguel. *Exploración del Río Grande o Nuevo Guapay, y fundación del Puerto de Higuerones.* Cochabamba: Imprenta de la Restauracion, 1873.

   Suárez Arana was Jefe Superior del Mamoré.

804. United States, Navy Dept. *Reports of Explorations and Surveys to Ascertain the Practicability of a Ship-Canal between the Atlantic and Pacific Oceans by Way of the Isthmus of Darien.* By Thomas O. Selfridge, Commander, U.S. Navy. Washington: Government Printing Office, 1874.

805. Venezuela. Direccton General de Estadística. *Memoria de la Dirección General de Estadística al Presidente de los Estados Unidos de Venzuela, 1873.* Vol. 3. Level, Andrés Eusebio. *El Delta del Orinoco tomado de la esploracion al alto bajo Orinoco y central en 1850.* Caracas, 1873.

   This is a report of the most thorough exploration of the Orinoco delta made up to that time.

806. Wagner, Moritz. *Naturwissenschaftliche Reisen im tropischen Amerika, ausgeführt auf veranlassung und mit unterstützung weiland, Sr. M. des königs Maximilian II von Bayern.* Stuttgart: J.G. Cotta, 1870.

807. Wiener, Charles. *Expédition scientifique francaise au Pérou et en Bolivie ..., 1875-1877.* Paris: 1879.

   The expedition explored the Ucayali and Huallaga rivers.

808. ———. *Pérou et Bolivie. Récit de voyage suivi d'Etudes archéologiques et ethnographiques et de notes sur ... les langues des populations indiennes.* Paris: Hachette, 1880.

   A very comprehensive work, containing over 1000 engravings and 27 maps.

809. Wilkes, Charles. *Narrative of the United States Exploring Expedition, Years 1838-1848.* 3 vols. Washington, 1854. Reprinted, Monticello, N.Y.:

Lubrick & Cramer, 1968.

Volumes 1 and 2 describe the surveying explorations along the southern South American coast made by this exploring expedition under Lt. Charles Wilkes, U.S.N., in 1839.

810. Wolf, Theodor. *Viajes científicos por la república del Ecuador, verificados y publicados por orden del supremo gobierno de la misma república....* 3 vols. in 1. Guayaquil: Imprenta del Comercio, 1879.

2. Secondary sources.

811. Barman, Roderick J. "The Forgotten Journey: Georg Heinrich Langsdorff and the Russian Imperial Scientific Expedition to Brazil, 1821-1829." *Terrae Incognitae,* 3 (1971): 67-96.

The definitive study of this expedition. Very well-documented; a work of solid scholarship.

812. Caro Molina, Fernando, ed. *De Agustín Codazzi a Manuel María Paz.* Cali, 1934.

Contains biographical sketches and some documents on the expedition headed by Codazzi to map and describe the country.

813. Dozer, Donald Marquand. "Matthew Fontaine Maury's Letter of Instruction to William Lewis Herndon." *Hispanic American Historical Review,* 28 (1948): 212-28.

Points out Maury's threefold interest in Brazil--scientific, commercial, and political; in the latter aspect he looked toward Brazil as a safety valve for U.S. slaves and their masters.

814. ———. "Path Finder of the Amazon." *Virginia Quarterly Review,* 23 (1947): 554-67.

The story of Lt. William Herndon's exploring mission to Brazil, well-told. There is no documentation.

815. Florence, Hercules. "Esboço de viagem de Langsdorff no interior do Brasil, desde Setembro de 1825 pelo 2.º desenhista da commissão scientífica Hercules Florence, traduzido por Alfredo d'Escragnolle Taunay." *Revista Trimensal do Instituto Histórico, Geográphico e Ethnográphico do Brasil*, 38 (1875): 355-441 (pt. 1), 231-301 (pt. 2); 39 (1976): 157-82 (pt. 3).

* García, Rodolpho. "Historia das exploracões scientíficas." Item 669.

816. Harrison, John P. "Science and Politics: Origins and Objectives of Mid-Nineteenth Century Government Expeditions to Latin America." *Hispanic American Historical Review*, 35 (May 1955): 175-202.

* Leitão, Cândido Mello. *História das expedicões científicas no Brasil*.

    Item 739.

817. Lesser, Alexander. *Survey of Research on Latin America by United States Scientists and Institutions*. Washington, 1946.

818. Macera Dall' Orso, Pablo. "Los viajeros franceses y el Perú Republicano (1826-1890)." *Revista Peruana de Cultura*, 5 (Abr. 1965): 50-70.

    Includes all the important French explorers, with a bibliography of their works.

819. Manizer, G.G. *A Expedição do Acadêmico G.I. Langsdorff ao Brasil (1821-1828)*. Ed. póstuma organizada por B.G. Xprintsin. Traduc. por Osvaldo Peralva. São Paulo: Editora Nacional, 1967.

    An excellent study; the work of a Russian ethnographer who came to Brazil in 1914-15.

820. Miller, Robert Ryal. *For Science and National Glory: the Spanish Scientific Expedition to America, 1862-66*. Norman: Universtiy of Oklahoma Press, 1968.

    The definitive study. An excellent work, well-written and thoroughly documented.

821. Núñez, Estuardo. "El Amazonas en el afán científico de los viajeros Herndon y Gibbon." *Cuadernos Americanos*, 113 (6) (México, Nov.-Dic. 1960): 188-202.

822. ———. "Over the Andes and Along the Amazon." *Américas*, 12 (March 1960): 27-31.

   A good, short account of James Orton's journey, with illustrations.

* ———. "Las viajeros de tierra adentro." *Journal of Inter-American Studies*, 2 (1) (1960): 9-44.

   Item 741. Covers the careers of foreign explorers of the nineteenth century, with particular reference to Americans.

823. Ponko, Vincent. *Ships, Seas and Scientists: U.S. Navy Exploration and Discovery in the Nineteenth Century*. Annapolis: Naval Institute Press, 1974.

   A work of careful scholarship, well-documented, with an extensive bibliography.

824. Rasmussen, Wayne D. "The United States Astronomical Expedition to Chile, 1849-1852." *Hispanic American Historical Review*, 34 (1954): 103-13.

   An excellent, well-written account of this expedition.

825. Reiss, Johann Wilhelm. *Herr Reiss: über seine reisen in Süd-Amerika*. Berlin, 1877. (Reprint from *Verhandlugen der Gesellschaft für Erkunde zu Berlin*. No. 5, 1877.)

   A good, brief description of his work.

826. Schumacher, Hermann Albert. "Agostino Codazzi en Bogotá." *Boletín Cultural y Bibliográfico*, 9 (1) (Bogotá, 1966): 111-16.

* Tafur Gracés, Leonardo. "Exploraciones y expediciones científicas a territorio gracolombiano...."

   Item 745.

827. Uzcátegui, Emilio. "Scientific Explorers in Latin America." *Américas*, 19 (July 1967): 3-11.

A good, very brief survey from La Condamine to the early nineteenth century. Illustrations.

E. Twentieth-century exploration.

1. Primary sources.

828. André, Eugene. *A Naturalist in the Guianas*. With a Preface by Dr. J. Scott Keltie. London: Thomas Nelson, 1912.

829. Bandelier, Adolphe. *The Islands of Titicaca and Koati*. New York: The Hispanic Society of America, 1910.

The work of a Swiss-American ethnologist and archaeologist.

830. Bingham, Hiram. *Across South America*. Boston and New York: Houghton Mifflin Co., 1911.

The earlier explorations of the man who discovered Machu Picchu.

831. ———. "In the Wonderland of Peru." *The National Geographic Magazine*, 24 (April 1913): 387-573.

This preliminary report of the discovery of Machu Picchu to The National Geographic Society and Yale University, co-sponsors, fills the entire April issue. There are numerous photographs and a map.

832. ———. *In the Wonderland of Peru: the Work Accomplished by the Peruvian Expedition of 1912, under the Auspices of Yale University and the National Geographic Society*. Washington: The National Geographic Society, 1913.

The complete report of the expedition's findings.

833. ———. *Inca Land; Explorations in the Highlands of Peru*. Boston and New York: Houghton Mifflin Co., 1922.

An expanded story of Bingham's explorations, including those subsequent to the discovery of Machu Picchu.

There is a good bibliography.

834. ———. *Lost City of the Incas. The Story of Machu Picchu and Its Builders.* New York: Atheneum, 1969.

   Based on his original publications, now out of print, and subsequent works of scholarship on Machu Picchu. Contains a good selection from the photographs taken at the discovery.

835. Cherrie, Goerge K. *Dark Trails*: *Adventures of a Naturalist.* New York: Putnam, 1930.

   A colorful account of his explorations, including his part in the Roosevelt-Rondon expedition (Part 6).

836. Costa, Craveiro. *A conquista do Deserto Ocidental (Subsidios para a História do Território do Acre).* Sao Paulo: Cia. Editora Nacional, 1940.

   Includes explorations in Acre and along the Bolivian border. There are an introduction and notes by Abquar Bastos.

837. Cowell, Adrian. *The Heart of the Forest.* New York: Knopf, 1961.

   Explorations along the Rio Xingu.

838. Delebecque, J. *A Travers l'Amérique du Sud.* Paris: Plon-Nournit et cie., 1907.

   A very interesting narrative of the journey of two brothers from Guayaquil across the Cordillera to the Río Ucayali, and down the Amazon to Belém.

839. Domville-Fife, Charles William. *Among the Wild Tribes of the Amazon. An Account of Exploration and Adventure on the Mighty Amazon and Its Confluents, with Descriptions of the Savage Head-Hunting and Anthropophagous Tribes Inhabiting Their Banks.* London: Seeley, Service & Co., Ltd., 1924. 2nd ed., Philadelphia: J.B. Lippincott Co.; London: Seeley, Service & Co. Ltd., 1924.

   An interesting account of the results of an expedition undertaken at the behest of *The Times* (London)

Nineteenth- and Twentieth-Century Exploration

expedition undertaken at the behest of *The Times* (London) and other papers in Britain and the United States. Good on the work of the Indian Service.

840. Duguid, Julian. *Green Hell. A Chronicle of Travel in the Forests of Eastern Bolivia.* London, 1931.

841. Dyott, George M. *On the Trail of the Unknown. In the Wilds of Ecuador and the Amazon.* New York: Putnam; London: Butterworth, 1926,

842. ————. "The Search for Col. Fawcett." *Geographical Journal,* 72 (1928): 443-38; 74 (1929): 513-540.

    Presents what seems to be the only logical solution to Fawcett's disappearance.

843. Fawcett, Percy Harrison. *Exploration Fawcett....* Arranged from his manuscripts, letters, log books, and records by Brian Fawcett. London: Hutchinson, 1953.

    The complete, bizarre story of Col. Fawcett's strange search for a "lost city" in the interior or Brazil. Also published as *Lost Trails, Lost Cities....* New York: Funk & Wagnalls, 1953. Only the title differs.

844. Fleming, Peter. *Brazilian Adventure.* New York: Scribners, 1960.

    The story of his search for Col. Fawcett. Verifies Dyott's theory as to his disappearance. (See Item 842).

845. Gheerbrandt, Alain. *Journey to the Far Amazon. An Expedition into Unknown Territory.* New York: Simon & Schuster, 1954. (Translated by Edward Fitzgerald from the French *L'expedition Orinoque Amazone, 1948-1950.* Paris: Gallimard, 1952.)

    An interesting, vivid, colorful account of the work of the expedition, very good on descriptions.

846. Hauthal, Rudolf Johannes Friedrich. *Reisen in Bolivien und Peru, ausgeführt 1908....* Leipzig: Duncker & Humblot, 1911.

A report of a geological expedition, with numerous illustrations and tables.

847. Hurault, Jean. "Une Chaîne de Montagnes Imaginaire: les Tumuc-Humac." *Revue Française d'Histoire d' utre-Mer*, 60 (219)(1973): 242-50.

    Field work done between 1947 and 1962 convinced Hurault that these mountains shown by Henri Coudreau on one of his maps (many were inaccurate) do not exist.

848. Kroeber, Alfred L. *Archaeolgical Explorations in Peru*. 3 vols. Chicago: Field Museum of Natural History, 1926-30.

    Covers explorations at Trujillo, the northern coast, and the Cañete valley.

849. Lange, Algot. *In the Amazon Jungle: Adventures in Remote Parts of the Upper Amazon River, Including a Sojurn Among Cannibal Indians*. New York and London: G.P. Putnam's Sons, 1912.

850. ———. *The Lower Amazon. A Narrative of Exploration in the Little Known Regions of the State of Para*. New York: G.P. Putnam's Sons, 1914.

    Profusely illustrated.

851. [Lange, Gunnar Anfin]. *River Pilcomayo Exploration 1905-06*. Buenos Aires, 1906.

    Contains eight maps in a portfolio.

852. Meyer, Hans. *In den Hoch-Anden von Ecuador, mit Bilder Atlas*. Berlin, 1907.

853. Miller, Leo G. "The Descent of the Rio Gy-Parana." *Geographical Review*, 1 (1916): 169-91.

    His experiences with the Roosevelt-Rondon expedition.

854. ———. *In the Wilds of South America: Six Years of Exploration in Colombia, Venezuela, British Guiana, Peru, Bolivia, Argentina, Paraguay, and Brazil*. New York: Scribners, 1919.

Nineteenth- and Twentieth-Century Exploration 147

This very interesting narrative contains 70 good illustrations. Chapters 13-16 cover the Roosevelt-Rondon expedition.

855. Missão Rondon. *Apontamentos sobre os trabalhos realizados pela Commissão de Linhas Telegraphicas Estrategicas de Matto Grosso ao Amazonas. Sob a direcção do Coronel de Engenharia Candido Mariano da Silva Rondon de 1907 a 1915*. Rio de Janeiro: Tipográphica do Jornal do Commercio, 1916.

 Published originally as a series of articles in the *Jornal do Commercio* in 1915.

856. Nébias, Arnaldo Otavio. "Bandeira Anhanguera--1937. Exploring the Valley of the 'rio das Mortes' and the Region." *Revista Brasileira de Geografia*, Ano II (Abr. 1940): 155-72.

 There is a useful map, and a collection of meteorological data.

857. Oppenheim, Victor. *Explorations--East of the High Andes from Patagonia to the Amazon*. New York: Pageant Press, 1958.

858. Pérez Triana, Santiago. *Down the Orinoco in a Canoe*. London: W. Heinemann, 1902.

 There is an introduction by R.B. Cunningham Graham. The author was the son of a former president of Colombia and had to escape in 1893; he could not leave by sea so had to take the river route. Of value chiefly for descriptions.

859. Perú. Junta de Vías Fluviales. *Ultimas exploraciones ordenadas por la Junta de Vías Fluviales a los ríos Ucayali, Madre de Dios, Paucartambo, y Urubamba; informes de los señores Stiglich, Von Hassel, Olives y Ontaneda*. Lima: 1907.

860. ———. *Vías del Pacífico al Marañón*. Lima: Imprenta La Industria, 1903.

 Contains the diary of the expedition.

861. Rice, Hamilton. "Further Explorations in the N.W. Amazon Basin." *Geographical Journal*, 44 (1914): 137-68.

The explorations of an American physician and surgeon whose work in South America spanned the first quarter of the twentieth century.

862. ———. "Notes on the Rio Negro (Amazonas)." *Geographical Journal*, 52 (1918): 204-15.

863. ———. "The Rio Branco, Uraicuera, and Parima. Surveyed by the Expedition to the Brazilian Guayana from August 1924 to June 1925." *Geographical Journal*, 71 (1928): 113-42, 209-23, 345-56.

This expedition was marked by the use of special radio apparatus and a hydroplane.

864. ———. "The Rio Negro, the Casiquiare Canal, and the Upper Orinoco September 1919-April 1920." *Geographical Journal*, 58 (1921): 321-43.

Proved that Humboldt had considerably underestimated the actual length of the Río Casiquiare.

865. ———. "The Río Uaupés." Geographical Journal, 35 (1910): 682-700.

Includes a detailed medical study of the Indians.

866. Roosevelt, Theodore. *Through the Brazilian Wilderness*. New York: C. Scribner's Sons, 1914.

The former president displayed uncharacteristic modesty in this personal account; for the full picture, it should be supplemented by the works of Cherrie (Item 835), Miller (Items 853, 854) and Zahm (Item 881).

867. São Paulo, Brazil (State). Commissão Geográphica e Geológica. *Exploração do littoral*. 2 vols. São Paulo: Typográphica Brazil de Rothschild & Co., 1915-20.

The work of an expedition headed by João Pedro Cardoso.

868. ———. *Exploração do rio Juqueryquerê*. 2 ed, São Paulo: Typográphica Brazil de Rothschild & Co., 1911, 1919.

The work of an expedition under João Pedro Cardoso.

869. ———. *Exploração do rio Paraná.* São Paulo: Typográphica Brazil de C. Gerka & Rothschild, Rothschild & cia. successores, 1907.

   This expedition, which concentrated on the area around the Rio Teitê, was led by João Pedro Cardoso.

870. ———. *Exploração do rio Peixe,* 1907. 2.a ed. São Paulo: Typográphica Brazil do Rothschild & Co., 1913.

   The work of an expedition headed by João Pedro Cardoso.

871. ———. *Exploração do rio Ribeira de Iguape.* São Paulo: Typográphica Brazil de Rothschild & Co., 1914.

872. ———. *Exploração do rio Teitê (barra do rio Jacaré-Guassú ao Rio Paraná) ... 1905.* 3.a ed. São Paulo: Typográphica Brazil de Rothschild & cia., 1930.

   The report was written by Gen. Jorge Black Scorrar.

873. Sievers, Wilhelm. *Reise in Peru und Ecuador ausgeführt 1909 von Wilhelm Sievers.* München und Leipzig: Duncker & Humblot, 1914.

   The work of a German geographer who explored in Venezuela, Ecuador, and Peru.

874. Smith, Anthony. *Mato Grosso, Last Virgin Land; an Account of the Mato Grosso, Based on the Royal Society and Royal Geographical Society Expedition to Central Brazil, 1967-69.* New York: Dutton, 1971.

   Exploration in depth of the flora, fauna, climate, soil, rocks, and human inhabitants, as part of a project to build a road 850 km. long through the jungle.

875. Suárez Arana, Cristían. *Exploraciones en el Oriente Boliviano.* La Paz: González y Medina Editores, 1919.

   Explorations made with the help of his father, Miguel Suárez Arana.

876. Triana, Miguel. *Por el sur de Colombia: excursión pintoresca y científica al Putamayo*. Prólogo de S. Pérez Triana. Paris: Garnier, 1907.

877. Up deGraff, Fritz W. *Head Hunters of the Amazon. Seven Years of Exploration and Adventure*. Foreword by Kermit Roosevelt. New York: Duffield, 1923.

   A lively tale of "some of the most fascinating--as well as the most wretched--days of my life." Valuable for his observations on natural history, although he was not a trained naturalist.

878. Zahl, Paul A. *To the Lost World*. New York: Knopf, 1939.

   The ascent of Mt. Roraima, by a naturalist.

879. Zahm, John Augustine (H.J. Mozans, pseud.). *Along the Andes and Down the Amazon*. New York: Appleton, 1923.

   A delightful and valuable account of the travels of this priest-explorer.

880. ———. *The Quest of El Dorado*. New York: Appleton, 1917.

   An interesting account of his travels along the route of the conquistadores.

881. ———. *Through South America's Southland*. New York: Appleton, 1916.

   Includes an account of the Roosevelt-Rondon expedition, in which he participated.

882. ———. *Up the Orinoco and Down the Magdalena*. New York & London: Appleton, 1910.

   An account of his explorations in Venezuela and Colombia, following the Orinoco-Meta-Magdalena route.

   2. Secondary sources.

883. Berril, N.J. "Sea in the Jungle--excerpt from *Journey into Wonder*." *Atlantic Monthly*, 190 (Aug. 1952): 60-64.

   By a Canadian zoölogist.

884. Coutinho, Edilberto. *Rondon, o Civilizador da Última Fronteira*. Edição definitiva. Rio de Janeiro, Brasília: Instituto Nacional do Livro, 1975.

885. Goodman, Edward J. "Twentieth Century Exploration of South America." Philip B. Taylor, ed. *Contemporary Latin America*, pp. 38-44. Houston: University of Houston Office of International Affairs, 1970.

886. Jahn, Alfredo. "La exploración científica del Occidente de Venezuela." *Revista del Colegio de Ingenieros de Venezuela*, Año 8, Nos. 78-79 (Oct.-Nov. 1930): 522-39.

887. Kigar, Paul D. "The Phantom Trail of Colonel Fawcett." *Américas*, 27 (4)(1975): 17-24.

   Discuss his discoveries along the Amazon and in the interior of Brazil, 1920-25.

888. Martin, F.O. "Explorations in Colombia." *Geographical Review*, 19 (Oct. 1929): 621-37.

   Explorations in the upper Guayabero region, June 1920 to February 1926, as well as the Cordillera Oriental south of Bogotá and the Río Meta.

889. Melbourne, W.H. "Exploraciones en el sur del Perú, 1954." *Boletín de la Sociedad Geográfica de Lima*, 78 (1961): 30-33 $1°/2°$ trim.

890. Naylor, Douglas. "South America Calls to the Explorer." *New York Times Magazine*, Nov. 1, 1931.

891. Oliveira, Euzebio Paulo de. "Expedição Scientífica Roosevelt-Rondon." *Geologia*. Annexo No. 1. Rio de Janeiro, 1915.

   Contains a map and table.

892. Pan American Union. "Twentieth Century Explorers in Brazil." *Bulletin*, 81 (March 1947): 169-80.

    The Roncador-Xingu expedition.

893. Prado, Eduardo Barros. *The Lure of the Amazon*. London: Adventurers Club, 1959.

    The author was a one-time guide to the Hamilton Rice expeditions.

894. Savoy, Gene. *Antisuyo. The Search for the Lost Cities of the Amazon*. New York: Simon and Schuster, 1970.

    Includes the discovery of Vilcabamba and Muyok Viejo.

ADDENDA

Discovery and exploration in general.

895. Galvão, Antônio. *The Discoveries of the World, from their First Original unto the Year of Our Lord 1555.* Reproduced with the original Portuguese text and edited by Vice-Admiral Bethune, C.B. London: The Hakluyt Society, 1862.

   Pp. 80-233 cover Spanish explorations in America. The author was governor of the Moluccas who, after his return to Portugal, the victim of calumnies, spent the rest of his life compiling an account of all known voyages.

896. Low, Charles Rathbone. *Maritime Discovery: a History of Nautical Exploration from the Earliest Times.* 2 vols. London: Newman & Co., 1881.

   A good survey, covering all the major voyages down to Capt. James Cook.

897. Riesenberg, Felix. *Cape Horn; the Story of the Cape Horn Region, Including the Straits of Magellan, from the Days of the First Discoveries, through the Glorious Age of Sail, to the Present Time....* New York: Dodd, Mead & Co., 1939.

   Well-researched, but little documentation. There are valuable appendices (including a list of the first fifteen circumnavigations), and good illustrations and maps.

Fifteenth- and sixteenth-century exploration.

898. Silberberg, Robert. *The Longest Voyage: Circumnavigators in the Age of Discovery.* Indianapolis: Bobbs-Merrill, 1972.

Based on standard works. Concerned chiefly with the earlier voyages, with a brief review of those after the 18th century.

899. Lester, Charles Edwards, and Andrew Foster. *The Life and Voyages of Americus Vespucius*. New Haven: Horace Mansfield, 1852.

   Pro-Vespucci; accepts all four voyages. Part II contains Vespucci documents, the travels of Marco Polo, Ojeda, and Nicuesa, a letter from Humboldt, and a genealogy of the Vespucci family.

900. Navarrete, Martín Fernández de. *Viajes de Américo Vespacio*. Madrid: Espasca-Calpe, 1941.

901. Vignaud, Henri. *Americe Vespuce, 1451-1512*. Paris, 1916. Pro-Vespucci. Supports the 1497 voyage.

902. Léry, Jean de. *Histoire d'un voyage fait en la terre du Brésil*. Edited with notes by Jean-Claude Morisot. Genève: Librairie Droz, 1975.

   The story of the voyage of this Huguenot refugee and some Genevans to Brazil in 1598; describes the land and the Indians, especially the Tupinambás.

903. Pérez Embid, Florentino. *Diego de Ordás, compañero de Cortes, y explorador del Orinoco*. Sevilla, 1930.

   Very well-documented; covers the exploration of the river by a large party.

904. Brosses, Charles de. *Histoire des navigations aux terres australes*. Amsterdam: Nico Israel, 1967. 2 vols. (Reprint of the 1756 Paris edition.)

   Covers all the voyages to Patagonia.

905. Levillier, Roberto. *Descubrimiento y población del norte argentino por españoles del Perú. Desde la entrada al Tucumán hasta la fundación de Sgo. del Estero 1543-53*. Buenos Aires: Espasa-Calpe, 1943.

   A good account of the discovery and settlement of northern Argentina from the north, and the establishment of a communication route with Perú.

906. Llaras Samitiar, Manuel. *El descubrimiento de la Patagonia. Recopilación de noticias y estudios, correspondientes al descubrimiento de la Patagonia.* Buenos Aires: Paredes, 1951.

907. Sarmiento de Gamboa, Pedro. *Viaje al Estrecho de Magallanes (1579-1584). Recopilación de sus relaciones sobre los viajes al estrecho y de sus cartas y memoriales.* Edición y notas de Angel Rosenblatt. Prólogo de Armando Bracen Menéndez. 2 vols. Buenos Aires, 1950.

   The voyage is well-described in the prologue.

908. Carneiro, Edison. *A conquista de Amazônia.* Rio de Janeiro: Ministério da Viação, Obras Públicas, Serviço de Documentação, 1956.

909. Garcés G., Jorge A., ed. *Colección de documentos inéditos relativos al adelantado capitán don Sebastián de Benalcázar, 1535-1565.* Quito: Archivo Municipal, 1936.

910. Bandelier, Adolph F. *The Gilded Man.* New York: Appleton, 1893.

   The story of El Dorado, well-told.

911. Friede, Juan. "La expedición de Sebastián Belalcázar a Santafé." Boletín de Historia y Antigüedades, 42 (Bogotá, 1955): 723-30.

   A very well-documented study.

912. Van Heuvel, Jacob Adrian. *El Dorado: Being a Narrative of the Circumstances Which Gave Rise to Reports, in the Sixteenth Century, of the Existence of a Rich and Splendid City in South America ... Including a Defense of Sir Walter Raleigh.* New York: J. Winchester, New World Press, 1844.

   One of the last attempts to defend seriously the existence of Lake Parima. Calls Humboldt's findings into question.

Seventeenth- and eighteenth-century exploration.

913. Jiménez de la Espada, Marcos. *Viaje del Capitán Pedro Teixeira a aguas arriba del río de las Amazonas, 1638-1639.* Madrid, 1889.

    A scholarly work, well-documented.

914. Yves d'Evreux, O.M. Cap. *Voyage dans le nord du Brésil fait durand les années 1613 et 1614.* With an introduction and notes by Ferdinand Davis. Paris & Leipzig: A. Frank, 1864.

915. Moog, Clodomir Vianna. *Bandeirantes and Pioneers.* Trans. by L.L. Barnet of *Bandeirantes e pioneros. Paralelo entre duas culturas.* 2.a ed. Rio de Janeiro: Globo, 1961. New York: George Braziller, 1964.

    A good account of the *bandeirante* movement, with an attempt to compare it to the American pioneers.

AUTHOR INDEX

(References are to item numbers, not pages.)

Abrahams, Enrique G. 277
Abreu, João Capistrão de 239-42
Abud, Katia María 230
Acarete du Biscay 431
Acosta, José de 101
Acosta Solís, Misael 654
Acuña, Cristóbal de 404
Adalbert, Prince of Prussia 604
Adams, Percy G. 137
Agassiz, Alexander 526
Agassiz, Elizabeth Cary 709
Agassiz, Louis 708, 709
Aguirre, Juan Francisco 476
Albion, Robert H. 47
Albornoz, Miguel 268
Alcedo, Antonio 82
Alexander, Hartley Burr 138
Almagia, Roberto 152, 193
Almeida, Washington Perry de 243
Altoaguirre y Duvale, Angel de 278
Alvear y Ponce de León, Diego de 477
Amat di San Filippo, Pietro 150
Amaya, Lorenzo 738
Americal Historical Association 1
Andagoya, Pascual de 275
Anderson, Gerald 280
Anderson Yeatmann, III 2

Andrade, Francisco 269
André, Eugene 828
Andresco, Víctor 281
Angelis, Pedro de 33
Anghiera, Pietro Martiro d' 29, 151
Antonina, Barão de 710-11
Appun, Karl Ferdinand 605
Arcila Robledo, Gregoria 453
Arciniega, Rosa 369
Arciniegas, Germán 139, 194-96, 347
Arias de Grieff, Jorge 655-66
Arias Divito, Juan Carlos 510
Ariza, Alberto E. 348
Arrubla, G. 125
Atkins, John 424
Avezac-Macaye, Armand d' 147
Azara, Félix de 478-82
Azevedo, João Lúcio d' 454-55

Baião, Antonio 50
Baker, John N.L. 51
Baldrich, Juan Amadeo 527
Ballester y Castell, Rafael 3
Ballesteros Gaibrois, Manuel 102
Ballesteros y Beretta, Antonio 112, 174, 282

Ballivián, Manuel Vicente 511
Bandelier, Adolph (e) F.
  140, 829
Banse, Ewald 657
Barbosa de Oliveira, Américo
  597
Barbot, Jean 336
Barcia Carballido y Zúñiga,
  Andrés González de 34
Barclay, William Singer 300
Barman, Roderick J. 811
Barros, André de 456
Barros Arana, Diego 113-14
Bates, Henry Wallace 606
Bayle, Constantino 141, 283
Beaglehole, John C. 52, 512
Bechamel, François 447
Beck, Hanno 658
Bellogín Garcia, Andres 370
Benson, Edward Frederic 215
Benzoni, Girolamo 103
Berchet, Guglielmo 15
Berger, Paolo 4
Berrian, William 11
Berrill, N.J. 659, 883
Bertrand, Alejandro 747
Berwick, Jacobo María del
  Pilar Carlos Manuel Stuart
  Fitz-James, 10th Duque de
  84
Biddle, Richard 301
Bingham, Hiram 830-34
Bishop, Morris 371
Bollaert, William 337, 748
Bonpland, Aimé 624
Borda, José Joaquín 457
Born, Franz 349
Botting, Douglas 660
Bougainville, Louise-Antoine,
  comte de 432
Bourne, Edward Gaylord 104
Boussingault, Jean-Baptiste
  Joseph Dieudonné 712
Bove, Giacomo 713-15
Boxer, Charles R. 400-01
Brackenridge, Henry M. 749
Brand, Charles 528

Brandenburger, Clemente 244
Brann, E.R. 689
Branner, John Casper 716
Brazil, São Paulo 458
Brazil, São Paulo (State) see
  São Paulo, Brazil (State)
Bresson, André 529
Breymann, Walter Norman 339
Brisson, Jorge 530, 750-51
Brosses, Charles de 900
Brownell, Henry Howard 54
Bruhns, Karl G. 661
Buarque de Holanda, Sérgio
  115, 414
Burckhardt, Carl Emanuel 717
Bürger, Otto 531
Burmeister, Hermann 532-33
Burmester, Luis Germán 340
Burney, James 55
Burns, E. Bradford 5
Burton, Richard F. 534
Byron, John 433

Caillet-Bois, Ricardo R. 440
Callander, John 35
Calmón, Pedro 120
Camacho Cano, Enrique 175
Camin, Alfonso 284
Caminha, Pero Vaz de 231
Cardozo, Manoel S. 415
Carneiro, Edison 902
Carreras y Valls, Ricardo
  176
Carvajal, Gaspar de 267
Carvalho, Joaquim Barrades de
  232-34
Casas, Bartolome de las 105
Casel, Pedro S. 198
Castelnau, Francis de 752
Caulin, Antonio 116
Cawkell, E.M. 117
Cawkell, M.B.R. 117
Chaffanjon, Jean 535
Chardón, Charles Eugenio 663
Charlevoix, Pierre F.X. 118
Cherrie, George K. 835

Author Index

Chikhachev, Platon Alexandrovich 536-37
Church, George Earl 409
Churchill, Awnshan 36
Cidade, Hernâni 50
Cieza de León, Pedro 119, 384
Cobo, Bernabé 106
Cochrane, Charles Stuart 538
Codazzi, Giovanni Battista Agostino 753
Coelho, José Ramos 16
Colombo, Cristofero 166-70
Colón, Fernando 171
Columbus, Christopher *see* Colombo, Cristofero
Columbus, Ferdinand *see* Colón, Fernando 171
Comitato Onoranze ad Amerigo Vespucci nel Quinto Centenario della Nascita 17
Conway, William Martin, Baron of Allington, 539
Cook, James 484
Córdoba Lazo de la Vega, Antonio de 485
Cortesão, Armando 85-86
Cortesão, Jaime 18, 55, 120 235, 245-46, 405, 416
Costa, Abel Fontuora de 153
Costa, Cândido 107
Costa, Craveiro 836
Coudreau, Henri Anatole 540-43, 754-60
Coudreau, Mme O. 761-65
Courte de la Blanchardière, René 426, 486
Coutinho, Carlos Veigas Gago 247
Coutinho, Edilberto 884
Couyoudmdjian, Ricardo 142
Cowell, Adrian 837
Crawford, Robert 766
Crevaux, Jules Nicolas 767
Cronau, Rudolf 108
Crone, G.R. 664

Cruz, Luis de la 544
Cutright, Paul Russell 665

Dainelli, Giotto 57
Dantín Cereceda, Juan 58
Darwin, Charles 607-09
Davies, Arthur 177, 199,216
Delebecque, J. 838
Demontézon, Fortuné 459
De Terra, Helmut 666-67
Descola, Jean 331
Destefani, Láurio H. 248
Díaz de Guzmán, Ruy 372
Dobritzhofer, Martin 434
Dojcsak, G.V. 668
Domínguez, Luis L. 364
Domville-Fife, Charles William 839
Dozer, Donald Marquand 813-14
Drake, Edwin Cavendish 38
Duguid, Julian 840
Dutcher, George M. 5a
Dyott, George M. 841, 842

Edwards, William H. 610
Ehrenreich, Paul Max Alexander 545
Ellis, Alfredo, Jr. 417
Encina, Francisco A. 121
Enciso, Martín Fernández de 87, 276
Engstrand, Iris H.W. 908
Erickson, Robert F. 513
Escragnolle Taunay, Affonso de 412-13, 418-19
Espinsoa Gómez, Carlos 460
Estellé, Patricio 142
Esteve Barba, Francisco 388
Expedición Austral Argentina 768

Falkner, Thomas 435
Fawcett, Percy Harrison 843
Federmann, Nikolaus 342
Fernández, Juan Patricio 444

Fernández de Castillejo, Federico 143
Fernández Piedrahita, Lucas 350
Fernández Reyna, Manuela 374
Ferriera, Alexandre Rodrigues 488
Ferreira, Vieira 249
Ferriera Reis, Arthur Cezar 514
Feuillée, Louis 489
Figuerdo, Fidelino de 59
Figueroa, Francisco de 445
Fitz Gerald, Edward Arthur 546
Fitz Roy, Robert 769-70
Fleiuss, Max 250
Fleming, Peter 844
Florence, Hercules 815
Fonseca, João Severiano de 547
Fontana, Luis Jorge 718
Forero, Manuel José 515
Forero Benavides, Abelardo 154
Foster, Charles 897
France, Ministères de la Marine et de l'Instruction Publique 771
Franco, Carvalho 420
Freycinet, Louis C. Desaules de 772
Frézier, Amadée Francois 490
Friede, Juan 19, 351-55, 904
Friederici, Georg 60
Fritz, Samuel 446
Froger, François 491
Frontaura Argandoña, Manuel 61, 429
Fúrlong Cárdiff, Guillermo 461-62

Gaffarel, Paul 251
Galvão, Antônio 62
Gandía, Enrique de 144, 178 200, 303-06, 373-74
Ganzemüller de Blay, María Luisa 6
Garay, Blas 20
Garcés, Modesto 548
Garcés G., Jorge A. 903
García, Casino 285
García, Rodolpho 669
García Franco, Salvador 155
Garcia Rosell, Ricardo 389
Gauss, Carl Friedrich 611
Gendron, Val 670
Gerstäcker, Friedrich Wilhelm Christian 549-53
Gheerbrandt, Alain 845
Giannechini, Doroteo 773
Gil Munilla, Ladislao 270-71
Gillespie, James Edward 63
Giraldo Jaramillo, Gabriel 7
Gómez Picón, Rafael 671
Góngora Marmolejo, Alonso de 122
González Suárez, Federico 123
Goodman, Edward J. 64, 145, 885
Graham, Robert B. Cunninghame 375, 390
Graterón, Daniel 356
Greenlee, William B. 252
Greve, Ernesto 321
Griffin, Charles C. 8
Grillet, Jean 447
Gropp, Arthur E. 9, 10
Groussac, Paul 305, 376
Grymaeus, Simon 39
Guedes, Max Justo 253-54
Guillemard, Francis H.H. 217
Guillot Muñoz, Alvaro 516
Gumilla, José 425

Habel, Jean 598
Haebler, Konrad 357
Haenke, Thaddaeus Perigrinus 492-94

Author Index

Hakespiel, Phil 672
Hakluyt, Ruchard 40
Hammerly Dupuy, Daniel 673
Hanson, Earl P. 65
Harcourt, Robert 343
Harlow, Vincent T. 286
Harrison, John P. 816
Harrisse, Henry 21, 306
Hartt, Charles Frederick 719
Haskins, Caryl P. 124
Hauthal, Rudolf Johannes Friedrich 846
Hawkins, Richard 365
Hawksworth, John 436
Heath, Edwin R. 774
Heawood, Edward 66, 398a
Hemming, John 391
Henao, Jesús M. 125
Henriques Leal, Antônio 463
Hernández Pinzón y Ganzimetto, José L. 255
Herndon, William L. 775
Herrera y Tordesillas, Antonio de 41, 108a
Hettner, Alfred 554-56
Hildebrand, Arthur Sturges 218
Hirsch, Lina 612
Holanda, Sérgio Buarque de *see* Buarque de Holanda, Sergio
Humbert, Jules 358
Humboldt, Alexander, Freiherr von 88, 613-24
Hurault, Jean 847

Im Thurn, Everard 625-26
Irving, Washington 179, 287
Italy, Reale Commissione Colombiana 22
Izaguirre Ispizua, Bernardino 464

Jahn, Alfredo 886
Jérez de Salamanca, Francisco 385

Jesuits, Letters from missions 448-51
Jiménez de la Espada, Marcos 410, 452, 776-80
Johnson, William Henry 67
Jos, Emiliano 241
Jouanen, José 465
Juan y Santacilia, Jorge 508
Julien, Charles-André 68

Kappler, August 557
Karsbein, Hermann 558
Kellner, Charlotte 675
Kerr, John Graham 627
Kerr, Robert 42
Keymis, Lawrence 344
Kigar, Paul D. 887
Kilpatrick, Frederick A. 332
Klencke, Hermann 676
Koelliker, Oscar 219
Kramer, Pedro 511
Kroiber, Alfred L. 848
Krüger, Paul 559-61

La Condamine, Charles-Marie de 495
Ladrillero, Juan Fernández de 317
Lafuente Machain, Ricardo de 377-78
Lagoa, João Antônio de Mascarenhas Judice, Viscondo de 220
Laguardia Trías, Rolando A. 307
Lange, Algot 849-50
Lange, Gunnar Anfin 851
Langnas, Izaac A. 156
Lapérouse, Jean-François de Galaup, comte de 496-98
Las Casas, Bartolomé de *see* Casas, Bartolomé de las
Latcham, Ricardo E. 146
Lawrence, Arnold W. 69
Ledesma Medina, Luis A. 378-79
Le Gentil, Georges 70

Leitão, Candido Mello 739
Leite, Duarte 126, 256
Leite, Serafim 466
Léry, Jean 328
Lesser, Alexander 817
Lester, Charles Edwards 897
Levene, Ricardo 127
Levillier, Roberto 201, 380-81
Lista, Ramón 562-65
Lizárraga, Reginaldo 109
Lizondo Borda, Manuel 382
Llaras Samitiar, Manuel 901
Lodares, Baltasar de 467
López, Vincente 128
López de Gómara, Francisco 318
López de Velasco, Juan 89
Low, Charles Rathbone 895
Lowe, Frederick 588

Macera Dall'Orso, Pablo 818
Macgillivary, W. 677
Magalhães, Basílio de 147
Magalli, Joseph 566
Magnaghi, Alberto 202
Makino, Miyoko 236
Malaspina, Alessandro (Alejandro) 499-502
Malheiro Dias, Carlls 23
Maling, D.H. 117
Manizar, G.G. 819
Marcondes de Sousa, Thomas Oscar *see* Sousa, Thomaz Oscar Marcondes de
Markham, Clements R. 273, 308, 322, 567-68
Martin, F.O. 888
Martínic Beros, Mateo 129
Martins Filho, Enéas 257
Martius, Karl Friedrich Philipp von 793
Mattos, Anibal 678
Maw, Henry Lister 569
McKinney, H. Lewis 679
Means, Philip Ainsworth 274

Medina, José Toribio 24-25, 221-22, 288, 308, 310-12, 323-24
Melbourne, W.H. 889
Melón y Ruiz de Gordajuela, Amando 223, 680-81
Menéndez, Francisco 437-38
Menendez, Raul 157, 441
Meyer, Hans 852
Meyer-Abich, A. 682-83
Middendorf, Ernst 570
Milet de Moreau, Louis-Marie-Antoine Destouff, Baron de 503
Miller, Leo G. 853-56
Miller, Robert Ryal 820
Mitchell, Mairin 224
Molinari, Diego Luis 180
Monnier, Marcel 571
Monteiro, Mario 313
Moog, Clodomir Vianna 907
Moraes, Rubens Borba de 11
Morales Macedo, Carlos 684
Moraks Padrón, Francisco 403
Moreno, Juan Carlos 442
Morison, Samuel Eliot 71, 158, 181
Morse, Richard A. 421
Motta, Avelino Teixeira da 86, 237
Moyano, Carlos M. 720
Moyano, María Clarisa 740
Mulhall, Marion 468
Muñoz, David 572
Muñoz, Juan Bautista 110
Murias, Manuel 50
Murphy, Robert C. 325
Musters, George C. 721-22
Mutis, José Celestino 427
Myers, Henry Morris 723

Naia, Alexandre Gaspar de 314
Navarrete, Martín Fernández de 43, 182, 225, 289, 898
Naylor, Douglas 890
Nebias, Arnaldo Otávio 856
Nectario Maria, Hermano 290

Nelson, Jean Thomas 471
Nieuhoff, John 329
Nodal, Bartholome Garcia de 439
Novo y Colson, Pedro de 517
Nowell, Charles E. 72, 148, 183, 203, 211, 258, 291, 315
Núñez, Estuardo 685-86, 741, 821-22
Núñez Cabeza de Vaca, Alvar 366

Oberacker, Carlos 599
O'Connor d'Arlach, Tomás 573
Ojeda, V.A. 600
Oliveira, Eusebio Pedro de 891
Oppenheim, Victor 857
Orton, James 784
Osculati, Gaetano 574
Ovando-Sanz, Guillermo 504
Oviedo y Baños, José de 359
Oviedo y Valdes, Gonzalo Fernández de 111

Pagan, Blaise-François de, Comte de Merveilles 411
Page, Thomas Jefferson 785
Palacios, José Agustín 786
Pan American Union 892
Parias, Louis-Henri 73
Parish, Woodbine 575
Parodi, Lorenzo R. 518
Parr, Charles McKew 226
Parramore, Thomas C. 519
Parry, John H. 74-75, 159-60
Pastells, Pablo 316
Pavie, Théodore 576
Peabody, George Augustus 577
Pedrosa, Manuel Xavier de Vasconcellos 204
Penrose, Boies 76
Pereira, João Baptista Borges 603

Peres, Damião 77
Pereyra, Carlos 687
Pérez Embid, Florentino 360
Pérez Triana, Santiago 858
Perú, Junta de Vías Fluviales 859-60
Peterson G., Georg 688
Philippi, Rudolph Amand 787
Pigafetta, Antonio 212-13
Pinheiro, J.C. Fernandez 161
Pinkerton, John 44
Pinto, Olivério M. Oliveira 601
Pizarro, Pedro 386
Pizarro y Orellana, Fernando 333
Plane, Auguste 578
Pocock, H.R.S. 392
Peoppig, Eduard Friedrich 628
Pohl, Frederick J. 205
Pohl, Johann Baptist Emmanuel 788
Pombo, José Francisco da Rocha 259
Ponce Sanguinés, Carlos 520
Ponko, Vincent 823
Pons, François Raymond Joseph de 579-80
Portillo, Pedro 789
Pôrto, Aurélio 469
Portugal 26
Portugal, Ministerio do Ultramar 78
Posada, Eduardo 629
Prado, Eduardo Barros 893
Prescott, William H. 393
Prévost, Antoine François 45
Puente y Olea, Manuel de la 90
Purchas, Samuel 46

Queiroz-Velloso, José María de 227
Quijarro, Antonio 581

Raimondi, Antonio 582, 602

Raleigh, Walter 345
Ramón Folch, José Armando de 326-27, 394
Ramos, Demetrio 292
Ramusio, Giovanni Battista 27
Randier, Jean 130
Rasmussen, Wayne D. 824
Ratto, Héctor R. 521
Reger, Fritz (Christian Friedrich Leopold) 583
Reiss, Johann Wilhelm 825
Restrepo, Daniel 470
Restrepo Tirado, Ernesto 361
Rey Balmaceda, Alfredo 742
Ricardo, Cassiano 422-23
Rice, A. Hamilton 861-65
Richman, Irving B. 334
Riesenberg, Felix 131
Rippy, J. Fred 471, 689, 743
Rivero, Juan 472
Rivero y Ustáriz, Mariano Eduaedo de 395
Rocha, Levy 690, 744
Roditi, Edouard 228
Rodrigues, José Honório 12
Romero, Carlos A. 32
Romoli, Kathleen 293-94
Roosevelt, Theodore 866
Rubio, Julián María 383, 443
Ruiz, Hipólito 505-06

Saint-Cricq, Laurent 584
Saint-Hilaire, Augustin François César Prouvençal de 630-41
Santos García, Brother 473
São Paulo, Brazil (State) 867-72
Sarmiento de Gamboa, Pedro 367
Savoy, Gene 894
Schaden, Egon 603
Schmidel (Schmidt), Ulrich 368

Schomburgk, Mortiz Richard 724
Schomburgk, Robert H. 725-33, 791-92
Schreibers, Karl von 691
Schuller, Rudolf 362
Schumacher, Hermann Albert 826
Schwarzenberg, F.A. 692
Seco, Carlos 206, 295
Severn, Derek 474
Shields, Robert Hale 149
Sierra, Vincente 132
Sievers, Wilhelm 585-86, 873
Silberberg, Robert 896
Simon, Pedro 338, 346
Simson, Alfred 587
Sinnhuber, Karl A. 693
Skelton, Raleigh A. 91
Smith, Anthony 874
Smith, Herbert H. 642
Smyth, William 588
Solnick, Bruce 260
Sousa, Thomas Oscar Marcondes de 162-64, 207-10, 261-64
Southey, Robert 133
Souza see also Sousa
Souza, Pero Lopes de 238
Spain 28-31
Spix, Johann Baptist von 793
Sprague, T.A. 694-95
Spruce, Richard 643
Squier, Ephraim George 589
Staden, Hans 330
Stange, Paul 561
Stanley, Henry Edward John Thomas, Baron Alderly 214
Steele, Arthur R. 430
Stefansson, Vilhjalmur 79
Steffen, Hans 794-802
Steinen, Karl von den 734-37
Steinmann, Gustav 590
Stephens, Henry 591
Sternberg, S. von 696

Author Index

Stevenson, Edward L. 92-94
Stoddard, Richard 697
Stoetzer, Carlos O. 698-99
Stuart, (Henry Windsor) Villiers 644
Stübel, Alfons 592
Suárez Arana, Cristián 875
Suárez Arana, Miguel 803
Suárez de Figueroa, Lorenzo 95
Sylva, Rafael 700

Tafur Garcés, Leonardo 522, 745
Taillemite, Etienne 507
Taunay, Affonso d'Escragnolle *see* Escragnolle Taunay, Affonso de
Teixeira, Pedro de 406
Ternaux-Compans, Henri 47
Thayer Ojeda, Tomás
Thouar, Arthur 593
Tobón Betancur, Julio 296
Torodash, Martin 13, 14
Torre Revello, José 523
Torres, Ana Palese de 746
Trevisano, Agnolo 172
Triana, Miguel 876
Tschudi, Johann Jakob von 395, 645-48

Ulloa, Antonio de 508
United States, Navy Dept. 804
Up deGraff, Fritz W. 877
Urteaga, Horacio H. 32
Uzcátegui, Emilo 827

Valdivia, Pedro de 319
Valentin, François 524
Van Heuvel, Jacob Adrian 905
Vargas Ugarte, Rubén 134, 428
Varnhagen, Francisco Adolfo de, Visconde de Pôrto Seguro 135, 186

Vasconcellos, Luiz Aranha de 407
Venezuela, Dirección General de Estadística 805
Verdoon, Frans 701
Vernon, Ida Stevenson Weldon 397
Vespucci, Amerigo 187-92
Viana, Francisco Javier de 509
Vidal de la Blache, Paul M. 96
Vigneras, Louis-Andre 165, 265, 297-98
Vila, Marco Aurelio 363
Villiers, Alan 702
Vindel, Francisco 97
Vives, Jaime Vicens 80
Vogt, John L. Jr. 266
Von Hagen, Victor W. 703-04

Wagner, Moritz 806
Waldeseemüller, Martin 98
Wallace, Alfred Russel 649-51
Wasserman, Félix M. 652
Waterton, Charles 653
Weise, Arthur James 81
Whitaker, Arthur P. 525
Whymper, Edward 594-95
Wied-Neuwied, Maximilian, Prine of 596
Wiener, Charles 806-08
Wilcox, Olive R. 79
Wilgus, A. Curtis 99
Wilkes, Charles 809
Williams, Edward F. 705
Wilson, Derek 398
Wilson, William Jerome 184-85
Wolf, Theodor 810
Woodcock, George 706

Ybot-Léon, Antonio 475
Young, Jean 69
Yves d'Evreux, O.M. Cap 906

Zahl, Paul A. 878
Zahm, John Augustine 879-82
Zárate, Agustín de 136, 320
Zuloaga, Guillermo 707
Zweig, Stefan 229

TOPICAL INDEX

Acuña, Cristóbal de, explorations 404, 405, 406, 411
Adalbert, Prince of Prussia, explorations 604
Agassiz (Louis) expeditions 708, 709, 719
Aguirre, Lope de 337, 338, 340, 341
Almagro, Diego de, explortions 326, 327, 380, 394
Amazon River and tributaries
  Discovery and early exploration 45, 124, 267-274, 335-341, 902
  17th century exploration 404, 411, 445, 446
  18th century exploration 446, 452
  19th century exploration 540, 542, 543, 545, 567, 569, 571, 581, 587, 588, 597, 604, 606, 610, 628, 642, 643, 649-651, 703, 704, 706, 734-737, 752, 754-765, 774, 775, 777-779, 784, 786, 813, 814, 820-822
  20th century exploration 835, 837-839, 845, 849, 850, 853, 854-856, 859-866, 876, 877, 879, 881, 891-894
America, Discovery
  Documents 15, 16, 21, 22, 27, 31
  Narratives 38, 39, 43, 69 70-72, 75, 81, 151, 152, 154, 157, 160, 161, 163, 165

See also Columbus, Christopher
Anchieta, José de 458
Andes: 19th century exploration 528, 539, 546, 569, 594, 595, 628, 654, 712, 717
  20th century exploration 852, 879
Anson, George, explorations 519
Appun, Karl Ferdinand, explorations 605
Argentina
  Documents 33
  History 127, 128, 132
  Early exploration and conquest 303, 305, 307, 372, 373, 375, 376-383, 901
  17th and 18th century exploration 431, 433, 435, 443, 461, 462, 487, 494
  19th century exploration 528, 532, 536, 544, 562-565, 573, 575, 591, 593, 713-715, 718, 720-722, 749, 768-770, 780, 809
  20th century exploration 851, 857
Azara, Félix de, explorations 478-492, 516

Balboa, Vasco Núñez de, explorations 277-279, 287, 288, 291, 293, 294
Bandeirantes 415-423, 907
Bates, Henry Wallace, explorations 606, 706

Bechamel, François, explorations 447
Belalcázar (Benalcázar), Sebastián, discoveries and explorations 903, 904
Bingham (Hiram) expeditions 830-834
Bolivia
  Early exploration 61, 148 379, 380, 429
  17th and 18th century exploration 520
  19th century exploration 539, 573, 581, 585, 752 773, 774, 786, 807, 808
  20th century exploration 840, 846, 857, 875
Bonpland, Aimé *see* Humboldt, Alexander von
Bougainville (Louise-Antoine) voyage 432, 507
Boundary Commission, Spanish-Portuguese, 1777 476-482, 487, 516
Boussingualt (Jean-Baptiste Joseph Dieudonné) expeditions 712
Bove (Giacomo) expeditions 713-715, 768
Brand (Charles) expedition 528
Brazil (*See also* Amazon R.)
  Bibliography 5, 11, 12
  History 115, 120, 126, 133, 135
  Discovery and early exploration 18, 53, 60, 230-274, 329, 330, 366, 370, 371, 425
  Colonization 23, 53
  17th century exploration and expansion 239, 400-402. *See also* Bandeirantes and Amazon R.
  18th century exploration 412, 414-423, 445, 446, 454, 458, 463, 466, 488, 491

  19th century exploration 533, 534, 547, 569, 571, 574, 630-643, 645-647, 649-653, 678, 708-711, 716, 719, 734-737, 739, 752 772, 788, 793, 813-815, 820-822
  20th century exploration 835-839, 847, 849, 850, 855, 857, 860, 874, 877, 879, 881, 891-893
Burmeister, Hermann, explotions 532, 533
Burton, Richard F., explorations 534
Byron, John, voyage 433, 436

Cabeza de Vaca, Alvar Núñez *see* Núñez Cabeza de Vaca, Alvar
Cabot, Sebastian
  Documents 25
  Biography and explorations 152, 165, 301, 306, 311
Cabral, Pedro Alvarez, discovery and explorations 39, 230-235, 240-242, 245-247, 250, 252, 253, 257-60, 262, 263
Caesars, Enchanted City of the 142-144, 146, 149, 378, 379-381, 437, 438
Carvajal, Gaspar de, exploration of the Amazon 267
Chaco Boreal, 19th century exploration 527, 627, 752
Chikhachev, Platon Alexandrovich, explorations 536, 537
Chile
  Documents 24
  History 113, 114, 121, 122
  Discovery and early exploration 317-321, 324, 326 388, 390, 392, 394, 397
  17th and 18th century exploration 437-439, 489, 490

Topical Index

19th century exploration 529, 544, 559-561, 591, 628, 747, 748, 787, 794-802, 820, 824
Codazzi (Giovanni Battista Agostino) expeditions 753, 812, 826
Coelho, Gonçalo, voyage 237
Colombia
  Bibliography 7
  Documents 19, 903
  History 125
  Discovery and early exploration 296, 351, 353-356, 361
  Conquest 60, 346-348, 350, 353-356, 361
  17th and 18th century exploration 427, 453, 457, 460, 470, 515, 522
  19th century exploration 531, 538, 554-556, 558, 583, 586, 619-621, 623, 629, 655, 656, 672, 677, 745, 750-752, 804, 812, 826
  20th century exploration 876, 879, 882, 888
Columbus, Christopher
  Bibliography 13
  Documents 22, 27, 166-170, 172
  Biography and voyages 39, 45, 165, 171, 173-185
Conquistadores 331-334, 346-362, 376-386, 388-397, 903, 904
Cook, James, voyages 52, 436, 484, 512
Cosa, Juan de la voyages, 281, 282, 284
Coudreau (henri-Anatole) expeditions 540-543, 754-765, 847
Cousin, Jean, voyage 161, 251
Courte de la Blanchardiére, René, voyage 426

Darwin, Charles, voyage and exploration 607-609, 663, 702, 704
Dávila, Pedrarias, explorations 275
Dias Pais (Fernão) expedition 415
Discoveries and early explorations
  English 286, 344, 345
  French 68, 251
  Portuguese
    Documents 16, 18, 26
    Histories and narratives 50, 56, 59, 77, 107, 153, 158, 163, 164, 230-248, 250, 252-254, 257, 260-263, 269, 291, 307, 313, 315
  Spanish
    Documents 22, 25, 27-31
    Histories and narratives 41, 43, 48, 62, 64, 65, 71, 72, 75, 80, 155, 248, 260, 269, 275, 277-285, 287-289, 291, 293, 294, 296-298, 300-303, 305, 308-312, 316, 327, 351, 361
Dombey, Joseph 505, 506, 510
Drake, Francis, voyage 387, 398

Ecuador
  History 123
  Discovery and early exploration 325, 452, 465
  19th century exploration 587, 594, 595, 600, 654, 655, 712
  20th century exploration 852, 873
Edwards, William H., exploration 610
Elcano, Juan Sebastián de, voyage 219, 224, 225
"El Dorado" 139-141, 349, 362, 905

Falkland Is. *see* Malvinas Is.
Fawcett (P.H.) expedition 841-844, 887
Federmann, Nikolaus, expedition 342, 255, 256, 353 *see also* Germans in Venezuela
Fernández, Juan, voyage 324
Ferreira, Alexander Rodrigues, explorations 488
Feuillé, Louis, explorations 489
Fitz Gerald, Edward Arthur, expeditions 546
Fontana (Luis Jorge) expedition 718, 738
French Orinoco Expedition, 1948-50 845
Frézier, Amadée François, explorations 490
Fritz, Samuel, Amazon explorations 446

Garay, Juan de, explorations 375, 383
Garcís (Aleixo) expedition 148, 313, 315
García de Moguer (Diego) expedition 312
Germans in Venezuela 60, 150, 342, 347, 355-358, 363
Grillet, Jean, exploration 447
Guerra, Luis, voyages 165, 265, 298
Guiana
  Discovery and early exploration 286, 336, 344, 345
  17th and 18th century exploration 343, 447, 459, 491
  19th century exploration 541, 542, 557, 625, 626, 724-733, 752
  20th century exploration 828, 878

Haenke, Thaddaeus Perigrinus, explorations 492, 499-502, 504, 511, 518, 520 *see also* Malaspina expedition
Harcourt (Robert) expedition 343
Haro, Cristóbal, voyage 302
Hawkins, Richard, voyage 365
Herndon and Gibbon expedition 775, 821
Horn, Cape 130, 131, 771
Humboldt, Alexander von, life and explorations 88, 611, 613-624, 629, 652, 654-663, 666-668, 670-677, 680-689, 692-700, 704, 705, 707

Im Thurn, Everard, explorations 625, 626

Jacques, Cristorño 243
Jiménez de Quesada, Gonzalo, explorations and conquest 348, 352-354
Juan y Santacilia, Jorge, explorations 508, 570

Keymis, Lawrence, explorations 344

La Condamine (Charles-Marie de) expedition 495, 508, 513, 704
Ladrillero, Juan Fernández de, voyage, 317
La Pérouse, Jean-François de Galaup, Comte de, voyage 483, 496, 497, 503, 524
Lepe, Diego de, voyage 271, 287, 298
Lista, Ramón, explorations 562-565
Lund, Peter Wilhelm, explorations 678

Magdalena R.
  Discovery and early exploration 348, 350, 351, 353, 354, 361

Topical Index

19th century exploration 656
Machu Picchu, discovery and exploration 831-834
Magellan, Ferdinand
  Bibliography 14
  Documents 24, 43
  Biography and voyages 45, 52, 211-229, 288, 300, 896
Magellan, Strait of 129, 131, 249, 300, 302, 303, 308, 309, 316, 367, 432, 439, 485, 491
Malaspina (Alejandro or Alessandro) expedition 492, 498, 500-502, 509, 510, 517, 518, 521, 523, 908
Malvinas Is. 45, 117, 304, 432, 440, 442
Mendoza, Pedro de, voyage 299, 305
Missionary explorers 444-475
"Monsoons," 412, 414
Moyano (Carlos) expeditions 720, 740, 746
Musters (George Chaworth) expedition 721-722, 742
Mutis, José Celestino 427

Natterer, Johann, explorations 691
Naturalists
  17th and 18th centuries 427, 430, 488, 489, 492, 499-506, 511, 515, 518, 520, 523
  19th century 557, 558, 599, 601, 604-707
  20th century 828, 835, 883
Nicuesa, Diego, voyage 287 298
Niño, Peralonso, voyage 39, 287
Nodal, Bartholome García de, voyage 439
Núñez Cabeza de Vaca (Alvar) expedition 364, 366, 370, 371

Ojeda, Alonso de, voyages and explorations 280, 283, 287, 292, 295
Ordaz, Diego de, explorations 285, 360
Orellana, Francisco de, discoveries and explorations 267-269
Orinoco R. and tributaries
  Discovery and early exploration 285, 286, 360
  17th and 18th century exploration 425
  19th century exploration 535, 805 *see also* Humboldt, Alexander von
  20th century exploration 845, 858, 882
Orton (James) expedition 723, 822

Pacific Ocean
  Discovery 275, 277, 278, 288, 291, 293, 294
  Exploration 52, 55, 71
Pampas, 19th century exploration 528, 536, 780
Pancaldo (León) expedition 374
Paraguay
  Documents 20
  History 118
  Discovery and early exploration 305, 313, 366, 368, 370, 371, 373
  17th and 18th century exploration 434, 444, 468, 480-482
  19th century exploration 591, 630-632, 752
Paraguay R., 19th century exploration 545, 767
Parima, Lake 145, 447
Patagonia
  Discovery 45, 52, 211-229, 288, 901
  17th and 18th century exploration 433, 435

19th century exploration
559-563, 565, 575, 714,
715, 718, 720-722, 740,
768, 770, 809
Pavón y Piménez, José Antonio,
explorations 505, 506, 510
Peru
Documents 28, 32
Early exploration and conquest 45, 119, 124, 134, 136, 322, 323, 325, 384-386, 391, 393
17th and 18th century exploration 426, 428, 430, 431, 464, 473, 486, 489, 490, 505, 506
19th century exploration 528, 529, 568-570, 572, 574, 578, 582, 585, 588-590, 592, 602, 615, 622, 623, 629, 648, 752, 790, 807, 808, 818, 820
20th century exploration 829-834, 848, 859, 860, 889, 894
Pinzón, Vicente Yáñez, voyages 39, 244, 255, 287, 289
Pizarro, Francisco, explorations and conquest 322, 384-386, 393
Pizarro, Gonzalo, explorations 274
Plata, Río de la and tributaries
Documents 33
Discovery and early exploration 45, 303, 307, 310, 311, 312, 314, 364, 368, 373-377, 383
17th and 18th century exploration 431, 378, 481, 487, 494
20th century exploration 869
Pohl, Johann, explorations 691, 788

Quesada, Gonzalo Jiménez de
see Jiménez de Quesada, Gonzalo
Raimondi, Antonio, explorations 582
Raleigh, Walter
Documents 29
Discoveries 286, 344, 345
Rapôso Tavares, Antônio, *see* Tavares, Antônio Rapôso
Rice (A. Hamilton) expeditions 861-865
Rojas (Diego de) expedition 378-382
Roncador-Xingu expedition 892
Rondon, Cândido 855, 884
Roosevelt-Rondon expedition 835, 853, 866, 881, 891
Roraima, Mt. 626, 878
Ruiz, Hipólito, explorations 505-506, 510
Ruiz de Andrade, voyage 323

Sabarabuçu 147
Saint-Hilaire (Augustin François César Prouveneal de) expeditions 630-641
Sarmiento de Gamboa, voyage 367-369
Schmidel (Schmidt), Ulrich, explorations 364, 368
Schomburgk expeditions 724-733
Scientific expeditions, official, 18th century
British 484, 512, 519
French 483, 489, 495-498, 503, 507, 513, 524
Spanish 485, 490, 499-502, 505, 506, 508-510, 517, 518, 521, 522, 523, 525, 908
Scientific expeditions, official, 19th century
Austrian 691, 788
Bavarian 788, 793, 806

Topical Index

Bolivian 773, 774, 786, 803
Brazilian (State of Pará) 754-765
British 766, 769, 770, 791, 792
Chilean 787, 794-802
Colombian 750, 751, 753, 812
French 767, 771, 772, 807, 808, 818
Peruvian 789
Russian 811, 815, 819
United States 749, 775, 784, 785, 804, 809, 813, 814, 817, 823, 824
Venezuelan 805

Solís, Juan de, discoveries and exploration 239, 243, 310
Souza, Pero Lopes de, voyage 238
Spain
 History 112
 Discoveries and early exploration *see* Discoveries and early exploration, Spanish
Spix and Martius expedition 788, 793
Spruce, Richard, explorations 643, 704
Squier, Ephraim George, explorations 589
Staden, Hans, explorations 330
Steffen (Hans) expeditions 794-802
Steinen (Karl von den) expeditions 734-737

Tavares, Antônio Rapôso, *bandeira*, 416 *see also* Bandeirantes
Teixeira (Pedro de) expedition 406, 408, 410, 411

Thouar (Arthur) expedition 593
Tierra del Fuego 439, 486, 714, 715
Tschudi (Johann Jakob von) expeditions 645-648, 690

Ulloa, Antonio de, explorations 508, 510, 525
Ursúa (Pedro de) expedition 337, 338, 341
Uruguay 409

Valdivia, Pedro de, conquest and explorations 287, 319, 321, 390, 392, 396
Vélez de Mendoza, Alonso, voyage 165, 265
Venezuela
 Bibliography 6
 History 116
 Discovery and early exploration 275, 280, 289, 292, 360
 Conquest 346, 347, 352, 356, 357-359, 363 *see also* Germans in Venezuela
 17th and 18th century exploration 424, 467, 472
 19th century exploration 535, 548, 579, 580 *see also* Humboldt, Alexander von
 20th century exploration 873, 878, 886
Vespucci, Amerigo
 Documents 17
 Biography and voyages 39, 98, 152, 186-210, 295, 897-899
Vieira, Antônio de 454, 456

Wallace, Alfred Russel, explorations 649-651, 679
Waterton, Charles, explorations 653
"White King," 148, 315

Whymper, Edward, Andean mountaineering and exploration 594, 595
Wied-Neuwied (Maximilian, Prince of) expedition 596, 744

Ref Z 1212 .G66 1983
Goodman, Edward J. 1916-
The exploration of South
 America

APR 2 3 1985